The Power of Employee Resource Groups

The Power of Employee Resource Groups

HOW PEOPLE CREATE AUTHENTIC CHANGE

Farzana Nayani

Berrett–Koehler Publishers, Inc.

Berrett-Koehler Publishers, Inc.
1333 Broadway, Suite 1000
Oakland, CA 94612-1921
Tel: (510) 817-2277
Fax: (510) 817-2278
www.bkconnection.com

Ordering Information

Quantity sales. Special discounts are available on quantity purchases by corporations, associations, and others. For details, contact the "Special Sales Department" at the Berrett-Koehler address above.

Individual sales. Berrett-Koehler publications are available through most bookstores. They can also be ordered directly from Berrett-Koehler: Tel: (800) 929-2929; Fax: (802) 864-7626; www.bkconnection.com.

Orders for college textbook / course adoption use. Please contact Berrett-Koehler: Tel: (800) 929-2929; Fax: (802) 864-7626.

Distributed to the U.S. trade and internationally by Penguin Random House Publisher Services.

Berrett-Koehler and the BK logo are registered trademarks of Berrett-Koehler Publishers, Inc.

Printed in the United States of America

Berrett-Koehler books are printed on long-lasting acid-free paper. When it is available, we choose paper that has been manufactured by environmentally responsible processes. These may include using trees grown in sustainable forests, incorporating recycled paper, minimizing chlorine in bleaching, or recycling the energy produced at the paper mill.

Library of Congress Cataloging-in-Publication Data

Names: Nayani, Farzana, 1977– author.

Title: The power of employee resource groups : how people create authentic change / Farzana Nayani.

Description: First Edition. | Oakland, CA : Berrett-Koehler Publishers, 2022. | Includes bibliographical references and index.

Identifiers: LCCN 2021055807 (print) | LCCN 2021055808 (ebook) | ISBN 9781523001248 (paperback) | ISBN 9781523001255 (pdf) | ISBN 9781523001262 (epub)

Subjects: LCSH: Organizational change. | Employee affinity groups. | Diversity in the workplace. | Industrial management—Social aspects.

Classification: LCC HD58.8 .N393 2022 (print) | LCC HD58.8 (ebook) | DDC 658.4/06—dc23/eng/20220103

LC record available at https://lccn.loc.gov/2021055807

LC ebook record available at https://lccn.loc.gov/2021055808

First Edition

30 29 28 27 26 25 24 23 22   10 9 8 7 6 5 4 3 2 1

Book production: Linda Jupiter Productions   Edit: Elissa Rabellino
Design: Frances Baca   Proofread: Mary Kanable
Index: Paula C. Durbin-Westby   Author photo: Aaron Jay Young

TO ALL WHO WISH TO BELONG AND THRIVE—
FULLY, WHOLLY, AND COMPLETELY.

· CONTENTS ·

· PREFACE ·

Do you remember the first time you heard about employee resource groups (ERGs) or got involved with one? I am always inspired hearing about the journeys of ERG leaders and members. My foray into the world of ERGs came as a result of my advocacy work in support of professionals of color. Many of these professionals were interested in building leadership skills and networking in order to uplift the cause of increasing diverse representation across the workforce. At the same time, they were committed to advancing their own careers and growing within their chosen fields of work. By bringing together employees with a common identity in support of an organization's diversity mission, ERGs seemed to be an elegant and natural way to achieve both of these goals at the same time. Not only would participating in an ERG help members of an underrepresented community gain skills, exposure, and experience at their company, but also, in furthering their career, they would help move the needle to directly and indirectly increase diversity at the highest level of leadership within organizations.

With that double-pronged mission in mind, I took up the mantle of leading a large professional association's programming, curriculum development, and advising on employee resource groups to corporate members and partners. This was both an honor and an immense responsibility over the years: to drive the gathering of thousands of attendees and executives from different industries and identities toward joint learning, sharing, and collaboration. I am grateful that I was entrusted with the opportunity to lead these initiatives, as it allowed me to deepen connections to the issues at hand and to the pioneering thought leaders in the space.

The more I was involved with convening summits and conventions related to employee resource groups—and sharing best practices through advising and consulting—the more I was exposed to how complex and impactful ERGs could be. I heard stories from various companies about how ERGs created immense impact and opportunity. As a public speaker and consultant on topics of diversity and inclusion, I have been fortunate over the years to have interacted with senior leaders and executives from Nielsen, Deloitte, Twitter, Bank of America, Clorox, The Walt Disney Company, Boeing, Wells Fargo, UPS, Bank of the West, SanDisk, Yelp, Google, the Central Intelligence Agency, Ernst & Young, and many more organizations. Hearing these senior leaders' most intimate stories and learning from what worked and didn't work, I started to mentally log best practices for ERGs that I could in turn share with others in my consulting work.

· With the connections made through ERG networks, and through my continued dedication to efforts to uplift voices and causes from the community, I was invited to visit, speak at, or work with organizations including Nike, Facebook, Walmart, AT&T, Coca-Cola, Toyota, Cisco, Amazon, Salesforce, eBay, BNSF Railway, Mattel, Experian, The McEvoy Group, LA Family Housing, and more. I had the opportunity to have one-to-one conversations with ERG leaders and their teams, learning about what projects they were working on and how they were optimizing their efforts for the common cause we all seemed to have: developing capacity to increase representation within leadership, enhancing our impact within organizations, and serving the communities that we represent.

Over time, I received special invitations to summits at the White House, cohosted with senior leaders in government, corporate, entrepreneurship, and nonprofit organizations. The dedication to meaningful change demonstrated by the participants at these gatherings was incredibly inspiring and propelled my understanding and commitment around ERGs to the next level. I continued to listen, learn, read, and observe. As I advised organizations, I passed on what I had learned from others, including the questions that were still collectively being answered. This sharing of best practices was particularly beneficial to many organizational leaders, as they were encouraged and motivated by what other organizations were endeavoring to do and how they had increased their effectiveness in achieving their defined goals. In the course of this book, I look forward to sharing with you the insights I have gained from these many initiatives, gatherings, and leaders.

At the same time that my interest and activities with ERGs were peaking, my work as a diversity, equity, and inclusion (DEI) consultant was evolving from advocacy for small business enterprise and minority entrepreneurship to focusing on supplier diversity. For a large part of a decade prior to my work with ERGs, I held a position as a business counselor in a program funded by the U.S. Small Business Administration (SBA)—a government agency that provides support to entrepreneurs and small businesses—and then later as part of a local chamber of commerce in Los Angeles. The SBA-funded Women's Business Centers across the country, like the one I was a part of, were magnets for minority business owners to seek resources and support. When I made the move from that program to the chamber of commerce, I became heavily involved in corporate supplier diversity initiatives, specifically with promoting educational events and cultivating opportunities for small business owners to do business with major corporations.

My contact with and appreciation for the world of minority certification and supplier diversity—which foster the participation of diverse entrepreneurs as suppliers to large companies and organizations—humbled me even further. There are so many ways that we can be involved with advancing diversity in the business world and beyond. My early experience with supplier diversity would later relate to how employee resource groups connect to diverse suppliers in the organizational context.

It was after doing all of that work that I was called to directly support large corporate organizations with DEI training and strategy. Previously, my main focus had been intercultural understanding and cross-cultural awareness training. Little did I know that my foundations in global and cross-cultural understanding would connect the dots through small business advocacy and DEI initiatives. It truly is cross-cultural understanding that is at the heart of all this work.

I am honored to continue giving back as an advisor to the Asian Leaders Alliance (ALA), a consortium of employee resource groups cofounded by ERG leaders at Salesforce and HSBC. I am inspired by how this alliance and other collectives of focused ERGs bring individuals together to share best practices and stories around how to pursue this work. Watching ERG pioneers give their time and talent to this cause is also what has motivated me to write this book: to create a resource that addresses questions and challenges that are commonly faced by employee resource group leaders and members.

This background story gives you some context about how I perceive the work with employee resource groups. It really is a coming together of several different and important parts of any business: workforce, workplace, marketplace, community engagement, and supplier diversity. These are the pillars I stand by in my work as a diversity, equity, and inclusion consultant, all built upon the foundation of intercultural understanding. The final stage of my professional journey includes diving deeper into personal development and coaching and exploring how healing is needed for true understanding, empathy, and transformational change within organizations. The challenging events of the current times related to systemic racial inequality, the visible needs of society amid a global pandemic, and my own personal search for connectedness to cultural healing practices have propelled the connection between DEI and the energetics of healing, in both my individual and organizational client work. I share more about this evolution of my perspective as we continue through this book.

I hope it is helpful to hear about my journey into the world of employee resource groups, and I encourage you to explore the influences that have taken place in your and your colleagues' lives, in order for you to reflect upon your own experiences and perspectives with ERGs. For me, it is through an all-encompassing approach to

DEI that I view employee resource groups. ERGs naturally represent the intersection of where these components of inclusion and belonging, equity, access, humanness, and personal growth come together. I have lived this intersection through my own journey within the DEI profession, community advocacy efforts, and practice of cultural healing. This multilayered experience is reflected in many of the lives of people I meet who are involved in this work, and it is at the core of how I interact with this work and my writing of this book. We cannot leave any part of our identities at the door when we enter a space. In the same way, when we enter the workplace, we take all of who we are with us. Employee resource groups help give those identities a home and a place to hang our coat. It is my hope that as you read this book, your own layers of identity and commitment to inclusion will be uplifted and reinforced with a sense of dedication, pride, and hopefulness.

Let us continue the journey together.

· INTRODUCTION ·

This book aims to present a holistic view of how employee resource groups exist in organizations and can organically serve multiple purposes within the company, while also impacting society overall. It centers the needs and perspectives of the people involved to connect back to the humanity that we are being called to embrace as we pick up the pieces of debris left after the challenges of global tragedy, heartbreaking racial oppression, and ideological polarization. The need for empathy and putting people first is at an all-time high. Organizations at all levels recognize that productivity cannot be attained if our people are not okay. And many of us are not okay. There is more that needs to be done.

While ERGs can address multifaceted challenges within an organization, we must remember to center the people involved and address their needs. Organizational leaders and ERGs can't do it all, nor can they accomplish all that is hoped for in the urgent time frame caused by heightened attention to tragic and emerging events in the world. However, deep transformational change can occur through incremental movements toward empathy and understanding combined with larger purposeful actions demonstrating commitment and focus.

This book, *The Power of Employee Resource Groups: How People Create Authentic Change*, takes us through how ERGs play a large role in the efforts toward organizational change—and how this is led by all people involved. We begin this book with chapter 1, outlining the types of resource groups and also the need for readiness within an organization and its leaders. Chapter 2 discusses the elements needed for organizational transformation and why change is needed now. Chapter 3 presents an overview of how ERGs can operate, utilizing the 5 Ps of effectively running an ERG. In chapter 4, we identify the key stakeholders involved with ERGs, addressing the people behind the purpose. From there, chapter 5 connects to organizational objectives and the key pillars of ERGs, and how ERGs can create and measure their impact. Chapter 6 emphasizes the importance of preserving space for community, solidarity building, and ERG relations among allies and supporters. Chapter 7 describes best practices and the common pitfalls that ERGs face. Chapter 8 explores potential opportunities and possibilities for ERGs through innovation, career advancement, alignment with community movements, and other new frontiers. Our final section, chapter 9, explores the future of ERGs within organizations and the power they have to continue transformational change.

These chapters include industry examples, quotes from ERG leaders, data from research publications, and commentary from industry experts, interspersed with my own narrative and personal experiences. I have also included illustrated models, as well as reflection activities and prompts that can be used to encourage conversation and purposeful decision-making among ERG leaders, to take the concepts we discuss in the book toward practical application at your own organization. At the end of the book is a glossary of key terms that may be helpful to reference as you move through the content and share these ideas with others. Terms that appear boldfaced in the text are explained further in the glossary.

It is my hope that in reading this book you are inspired by what has inspired me over these many years working with employee resource groups, and you will be equipped with the knowledge and tools to address key issues and overcome common challenges. Know that you are not alone. This work is a continuous process, and ERGs themselves often iterate and change over time, just as we ourselves evolve in our understanding of this work. I invite you to immerse yourself in this book as if you are in conversation with a trusted confidant who is sharing with you the secrets of how ERGs operate, what to watch out for, and how your resource group can benefit from the knowledge and best practices developed by others over time. Thank you for your commitment to serving your community and organization, and to impacting society as a whole. Your work is creating a legacy that will last into the future, and we are all better off for it.

ONE

ERGs, ARE YOU READY?

GETTING STARTED ON THE ERG JOURNEY

Networks of individuals have been present within organizations for decades in the form of affinity groups, employee resource groups (ERGs), employee networks, business resource groups (BRGs), employee councils, diversity councils, and inclusion councils.[1] The first known ERG, called the National Black Employee Caucus, was formed in 1970 at Xerox, with the support of Xerox's CEO at the time, Joseph Wilson. This ERG evolved from race-based employee groups at Xerox that emerged due to racial tensions in the 1960s to address discrimination and to advocate for an equitable workplace environment.[2] Since then, ERGs have formed within the workplace to support and represent people with identities and demographics related to gender, race, sexual orientation, ability/disability, caregiver role, military status, religious affiliation, generation, geographic area, job function, and more. For the purpose of discussion in this book, we will collectively refer to all types of employee groups as ERGs. ERGs have evolved into powerful sources of employee activity and engagement that organizations have leveraged to support business goals.[3] ERGs exist in many corporations across a wide array of industries, and yet in other companies they are still being founded. Among these are organizations that recognize the importance of ERGs but need help getting started.

Organizations that launch and support the operation of ERGs have differing needs. For some, it is the goal of increasing ongoing engagement with ERG members and alignment with the company bottom line. This could take the form of encouraging employee participation in internal diversity initiatives and support of sales and marketing efforts focused on diverse communities. For others, it is connecting with the overarching goals of leadership and making a case for why ERGs support existing organizational objectives—traction for action. At companies such as tech start-ups, individuals with little to no experience and knowledge about HR or DEI work are sometimes tasked with founding ERGs. Since the companies are new themselves, there is a lack of institutional history to draw on, which highlights an urgent need for guidance on how to begin. At higher education institutions, affinity groups exist on campus yet many are siloed and could be supported more effectively with guidance and a wider vision for their purpose and potential impact.

ERGs have been and remain a hot topic because of the omnipresent need to (a) engage employees; (b) organize events, initiatives, and programs effectively; and (c) continually justify their existence (and funding) to executive leadership within organizations. If these elements are not fulfilled, ERGs will fail. ERGs are constantly under pressure to showcase performance to senior leaders or their budgets will get slashed. At the same time, ERG leaders may feel drained, as if this is another job. There is therefore a delicate balance in how to support ERGs for optimal output without burning out the ERG members and leaders along the way. The issue of needing to balance responsibilities of the ERG role along with workplace duties is exacerbated with the greater context of the ongoing movements for racial justice and overall call for inclusion and equity within organizations. These factors may be compounded due to external forces such as the pandemic and needing to connect virtually and continue to build community and support employees, despite social distancing.

As we can see, there is a lot of terminology around employee resource groups, employee networks, affinity groups, and business resource groups. What are the differences between these groups, and which is appropriate for your organization?

AFFINITY GROUPS *are a gathering of individuals based on an identity demographic, such as race, gender, sexual orientation, military status, parental status, or other identity characteristic. Affinity groups come together as a collective of individuals to share experiences and offer support to one another around the common identity that is shared. Affinity groups can be found in companies, higher education institutions, schools, and other organizations that have the need to support individuals of underrepresented or underserved populations. Affinity groups are known for the ability to hold space for individuals who need support and create community building within the group and across other groups.*

Similar to affinity groups, **EMPLOYEE RESOURCE GROUPS** *are designed to support employees who share a common identity, but with a greater explicit connection to an organization's goals regarding inclusion, equity, belonging, and efforts to support employees overall. With employee resource groups, the affinity component of connecting individuals and offering support to employees through a network is intertwined with broader organizational commitments to diversity and representation. Organizational goals come into play when there is clear alignment between the employee resource group and the organization's stated DEI objectives.*

Taking the groups' relationship with the organization one step further, **BUSINESS RESOURCE GROUPS** *are squarely aligned with the business and directly serve purposes set forth by the organization to fulfill certain company needs. Some of these business resource groups are professional networks or may involve an identity trait or a characteristic more to do with the business. An example of a business resource group could be a network of women engineers. This resource group is specific to both identity and the role and function within the business. The terms employee resource group and business resource group are sometimes used interchangeably, but they do denote varying degrees of focus on business objectives. Some companies have employee resource groups and also employee networks, and membership in these groups is defined differently, depending on the purpose of the group. Each organization determines parameters around the purpose and membership of each group.*

Some leaders envision the progression of these groups as moving from affinity group to employee resource group to business resource group, in a linear way. Although that may be the case for some companies, that is not the case for all organizations. Some affinity groups do not move into serving employee and business functions. Also, employee resource groups may contribute to some functions of business but be centered around serving the employees' interests and needs. A more organic way of looking at the relationship between these groups and the organization is that each of these groups serves many functions at the same time.

A thought-provoking ERG model that conceives of the flow between functions and groups within organizations is the wave model created and conceptualized by Rodney Hill and Jimmy Hua on behalf of the Asian Leaders Alliance. This wave model, "ERGs in Motion," shows how there is a constant interplay between the different outcomes of ERGs and also impacts that ERGs have on society through advocacy, philanthropy, employee engagement, and more (see figure 1). The wave form illustrates the way that the community also builds momentum for organizational outcomes to happen. At the same time, societal forces can cause the need for organizations to respond to external factors.

The wave graphic is helpful in showing how ERGs are in a constant flow between various parts of the business in their purpose,

FIGURE 1. *ERGS IN MOTION.*
(SOURCE: RODNEY HILL AND JIMMY HUA, ASIAN LEADERS ALLIANCE.)

as well as the range of what they offer as value to the organization at any given time. Actions by ERGs can create increasing momentum for transformation and impact within organizations and in society overall, resulting in workplace engagement and the experience of value by the employee. This leads to advocacy within the organization and, externally, philanthropic efforts, which all connect to business value. Figure 1 depicts how impact can happen in all of these ways and, at the same time, how powerful movement always comes back to and begins with the community and culture of the people whom the ERG represents. This view may be preferable to linear models that show a progression from affinity group to employee resource group to business resource group because it demonstrates the ebb and flow of interest, engagement, effort, and impact that ERGs naturally cycle through. A linear model simply cannot apply to all organizations, for many organizations do not see their current state as a phase in evolution but rather consider their current state to be most suited to the makeup of the organization. Perhaps this model may resonate with your company leadership and ERG to capture the ongoing movement and efforts that are taking place at the same time with your ERG.

Reflect on the following: What goals and actions in your ERG create collective momentum for your group? What is the impact of the actions taken by your ERG, both internally to your organization and externally to the public? How does this impact flow back into strengthening both the business and the organizational culture and employee engagement through your ERG leaders and members? The power of employee resource groups is vast. The outcomes of actions taken by the group are far-reaching and can in turn reinvigorate the group and culture of the organization as a whole.

Who can be a part of employee resource groups? A common question that is asked is if someone who is not a member of the identity can join the affinity or employee resource group. Due to legal, nondiscrimination requirements, all employee resource groups must be open to everyone at the company. There is no limit

> Having allies and friends of an employee resource
> group is essential, and at the same time the focus
> should be on the functioning of the group to support
> those of the individual marginalized identity.

on which groups one can join and how many one can participate in. That said, it's important to notice when a person who is not of the identity is taking up space at an event or within the organizing leadership of the employee resource group. Having allies and friends of an employee resource group is essential, and at the same time the focus should be on the functioning of the group to support those of the individual marginalized identity. Educating allies and partners of the employee resource group can happen with the members of the group and also separately from the group. There is an opportunity to host events open to all and also ones that are focused on the identity characteristic, to preserve space and allow for dialogue among group members.

Diversity councils, also known as inclusion councils, are a company function consisting of leadership from across the organization and with clear objectives related to overall diversity, equity, and inclusion strategy. A diversity council can be a favored structure to include individuals of many backgrounds from different parts of the business, and they sometimes exist in replacement of employee resource groups. A few years ago, Deloitte made the news for choosing to disband its employee resource groups in favor of inclusion councils.[4] The primary reasons for this change were to be more inclusive of White male leaders and also to address millennial employees who felt that they belonged to more than one group, that they wanted to focus more on the professional experience at the company, and that Deloitte had a focus on cultivating an inclusive environment overall. This decision caused much dialogue in the DEI and ERG community as leaders were forced to reflect on their own ERG functioning and make the case for why employee resource groups were still a valid and preferred structure at their own companies. Deloitte explained that it was emphasizing the need for a more integrated, inclusive, and equitable environment in the general workplace, rather than siloing people into categories and groups.

An argument could be made that all organizations should take this stance and aspire to have DEI fully integrated in every aspect of the business. However, data and the personal experience of many employees show that the full spectrum of inclusion, equity, and belonging is not in evidence across organizations. There's a lack of representation at the highest ranks of all organizations, regardless of industry. There continues to be a strong rationale for DEI and employee resource groups. Historically excluded and underserved groups still face the systemic impacts of bias and discrimination that have limited their presence within companies in many ways. And we exhibit **survivorship bias** by focusing only on those who are currently present in an organization and overlooking those who left or never gained admission in the first place. This means that we may never know the full story of how many candidates could or should have been at organizations and instead were unconsciously made to feel unwelcome or were consciously excluded due to practices that eliminated access and their ability to be present.

As a result, the need for employee resource groups and affinity networks remains. ERGs enable individuals to convene around their identity and find comfort in common encounters of this shared experience. Employee resource groups serve as a source of support and often are the place where DEI initiatives take hold. Organizations would be wise to focus on employee resource groups as a means of connecting with employees who normally may not have a voice or visibility in organizational functioning. The collective insights and might of employee resource groups are a powerful resource to guide companies toward becoming a preferred place to work and also to operate more inclusively for all employees.

By weaving a culture of inclusion directly into organizational structures, ERGs offer the promise of more activated and engaged employees, who in turn can provide a significant boost to corporate activities in many areas, such as sales and marketing, product development, recruiting and retention, and community relations. The question at hand is: How can organizations prepare to benefit from the potential that employee resource groups have to offer?

ORGANIZATIONAL READINESS

As you consider the approach your organization takes toward ERGs, one critical item to consider is the readiness of your organization to engage in DEI work in general, and to launch and support ERGs specifically.

Seramount (formerly known as Diversity Best Practices) published a model called "Six Stages of Organizational D&I Assessment," which discusses the stages and evolution that an organization may be in with regard to diversity, equity, and inclusion work.[5] Examine where your organization falls on this continuum, as an organization that is focused on compliance and legal requirements will have a very different strategy and set of expectations than those of an organization that integrates DEI philosophy into the mission of its functioning and decision-making. The first stage, "Irrelevant," shares how there is a "limited focus" on this work, with EEO (Equal Employment Opportunity) and regulatory compliance-driven measures as the only ways that diversity is addressed, if at all. The second stage, "Awareness," is focused on "improving morale," although the DEI team has limited influence. The third stage, "Discovery," is described as "Leaders Getting It," whereby leadership starts to see the value and relevance of the work and begins to commit resources. The fourth stage, "Application," is characterized by the creation of DEI programs and embedding DEI process, but application of this is done narrowly, only to issues of people and culture. The fifth stage, "Integration," focuses on "Embedding D&I into Organization" and HR strategies. The final stage, "Realization," demonstrates "D&I as a Valuable Business Asset," focusing on how DEI efforts contribute to business growth in a measurable way. The focus on organizational readiness for DEI can help guide leaders as to whether they should continue focusing on overall organizational development in preparation for launching ERGs.

There is justifiably a lot of attention paid to the organizational readiness of a company to hold diversity, equity, and inclusion initiatives within the organizational context. However, what about the readiness of the leaders themselves? In my work doing consulting with a variety of different clients, I have found that leaders' DEI readiness is a big key factor in the success of any DEI initiative. There are individuals who are able and willing to lead the initiatives, and there are others who are supportive but need further education. There are also others who are on board but are not as responsive. Finally, there is a group of people who may be resistant to any DEI effort or to organizational change in general.

To address the different viewpoints and approaches to DEI found within organizations, I have created the "DEI Stakeholder Disposition" framework, which charts these various stakeholders in terms of their positioning toward diversity, equity, and inclusion (see figure 2). This DEI Stakeholder Disposition chart is a useful tool for organizations to assess where their DEI stakeholders fall. As you plan

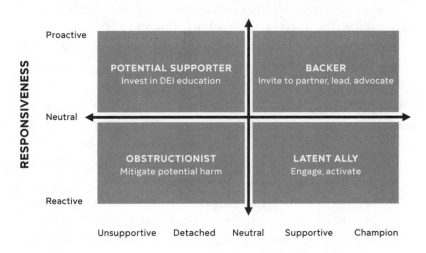

FIGURE 2. *DEI STAKEHOLDER DISPOSITION.*

your employee resource group and DEI strategy overall, it is important to acknowledge where individuals stand in terms of approaching diversity, equity, and inclusion.

The key is to acknowledge where individuals' disposition may fall and also their responsiveness level to diversity, equity, and inclusion initiatives. First, you have "Potential Supporters," who are proactive in addressing DEI issues but may be detached from or unaware of the potential impact of the effort. The best method to support this group is to invest in further education, awareness building, dialogue, and coaching, which can help the individual to move through learning and understanding about these initiatives. Second, you have individuals who are "Backers" of the cause. They are proactive champions of DEI efforts and are highly willing to engage and respond around DEI efforts. The third group can be described as "Obstructionists." These are individuals who are resistant to change, or less involved in the effort, and may actually become roadblocks to the progress of diversity, equity, and inclusion efforts at the organization. We must explore why and how a person moved into this disposition. They could have arrived at this place due to previous DEI efforts that were unsuccessful or caused greater harm. Or, they may not feel that this effort is going to lead anywhere. It is critical to hold space for these individuals and address concerns they have, especially in order to mitigate harm that may be caused by their lack of participation in the process. The final category is "Latent Ally." These are individuals who are champions of the cause but are less responsive. Perhaps they do not know how to approach the situation or—fearful of unintentional wrongdoing—yield to others to make decisions or are paralyzed due to the wide range of options before them.

In any organization or group, there is a combination of all these dispositions at the same time. That is what makes DEI efforts so challenging! If we erroneously believe that we can layer a single DEI strategy on top of an organization and find success, this blanket approach will lead to failure. It is necessary to have an overall

....

A blanket approach to DEI efforts at organizations will lead to failure.

....

strategy for the organization as well as to acknowledge and honor individual experiences within the DEI process that could likely be different for everyone.

Numerous factors shape a person's DEI disposition. One is trust in the organization. If there have been previous efforts that have failed, that can leave a bad taste in the mouth of any individual who is approached with a new effort. I have seen time and again how prior DEI initiatives that failed have left company employees with a lack of trust, hope, and faith in the process. Or, inadequate responsiveness leading up to a formalized DEI effort means that individuals may be cautious with any new DEI initiative. Also, the pressure and context of societal events impact individuals' ability to show up to this process, because it may be triggering and retraumatizing for individuals who have already gone through pain and suffering from their own personal identity being marginalized outside of work. Why would they want to engage further in this at work? This is the case for many people of marginalized identity groups who do not have much left to give toward efforts to create an inclusive and equitable space that they may perceive is not something they have power or responsibility to design, anyway.

Given that, we must be mindful not to create further harm in individuals who have already experienced systemic discrimination or othering. Asking them to show up to a process without the space to process their own emotions, and any encounters related to their identity, overlooks their authentic experiences. Also, being overly hopeful and optimistic about the DEI efforts, when past track records within the company or society at large have been less than favorable, is a form of **toxic positivity**. This toxic positivity can railroad any effort toward diversity, equity, and inclusion because it showcases how the goal of success of the DEI effort as a strategy is more important than the experience of individuals in the effort. It may be perceived as overlooking the true experiences of individuals who have had less-than-positive encounters with this work. This holds true for individuals who don't see value in DEI work at all. There is a large number of people who may feel that the workplace is of equal opportunity to all, so therefore we should just consistently pay attention to workplace objectives, and any individual who is an optimal performer will thrive. This perspective is quite common in organizations and requires careful communication and open dialogue to help bring forth understanding about how systemic dynamics of historical exclusion of certain populations and overarching bias within processes and individual interactions have led to inequitable workplaces as a whole.

Another issue that affects a person's DEI disposition is the idea of allyship. Allyship has grown to be a term that has morphed into an idealized state that many people feel they cannot reach. I have been told by many individuals who are engaged in DEI work that they don't feel they can call themselves allies because they still make mistakes and don't know what to do in many situations. Also, they may feel they are being monitored by other individuals to see if they are making a misstep in the work. Both of these experiences lead to the disposition of a latent ally. A latent ally is someone who is truly engaged and inspired to do the work but can often be paralyzed and feel unable to act. This can be detrimental to the process because in moments when there needs to be advocacy and action—and latent allies may feel hesitant to step up—the burden of the experience falls onto a few key leaders who are constantly doing the work for the entire group.

"Potential supporters" are a key group because there are people who are not fully engaged in understanding the magnitude or potential impact of the work, but they are highly responsive to the efforts and could benefit from learning more. Perhaps they are detached from the effort because it is not in their wheelhouse of expertise or lived experience. Or, they don't have an entry point to get involved.

Potential supporters are a large opportunity for a network to tap, to support DEI and employee resource group efforts. These are potential partners who can aid in the cause and can help move the masses of individuals who are highly unlikely to be directly involved in the efforts. We should not forget these individuals who fall under the group of potential supporters, as they can contribute much to the effort in terms of resources, guidance, and also feedback that can be instrumental in its success across the organization.

DEI backers are individuals who are completely involved in the process and understand the impact and urgency of any issue. They may have the resources, funds, bandwidth, and awareness level to be able to take on this level of engagement. However, we must be mindful that DEI backers may burn themselves out if only they and not others in the other three categories are doing the work. Also, if efforts are led only by the DEI backers, it is actually a smaller population than members of the general group, who are all at different levels of being on board. To succeed in the long run, DEI work must reflect the reality of the entire body of an organization's members and incorporate their collective points of view. The process itself must reflect the goal of inclusion.

Successfully starting and sustaining a DEI campaign in an organization is a complex and multilayered effort. In addition to developing an impactful DEI strategy, attention needs to be paid to the individuals who are part of the work, where they are at in terms of their DEI disposition, their identity and lived experience, the wherewithal they have for the work, and the resources that are available to individuals and groups. This is how deep organizational change and transformation takes place. Policies and practices definitely support DEI efforts—however, what guarantees the success of any DEI effort are the people involved. People are what create organizational culture. Without people, any externally enforced mandate or internally inspired effort will not be successfully implemented in a way that is visible, measurable, and sustainable. It is the people who create authentic change. Or who can be resistant to it. Both are true at the same time.

....

DEI work is a moving landscape, and the people within it are also growing and changing at every turn.

....

At every turn, we must be mindful and aware of where our colleagues, partners, and leaders are at, in terms of their DEI disposition at any given time. They may be backers one day but need to take a break and become latent allies the next day, depending on their bandwidth or other competing stressors and priorities. Some individuals could be the biggest resistors and obstructionists but then move along toward becoming advocates and partners. DEI work is a moving landscape, and the people within it are also growing and changing at every turn. You may lose supporters if you adopt policies that are more inclusive to some individuals and less inclusive to others. You may also gain traction if you have a big win around a cause that appeals to a wider identity group in addition to the demographic of your own employee resource group. DEI and employee resource groups need to be strategic and intentional, centering the needs and experiences of people as a core value of any initiative that is implemented.

At the same time, one cannot overlook the need to connect with business objectives. Employee resource groups sit within an organizational context. As much as social causes and societal activism need to be integrated into organizational activities, employee resource groups must align with organizational objectives and vice versa, in order to fully thrive and be sustainable in the long term. I have witnessed many instances of expectations set by the employee resource group or by the organization that were unfeasible and unreasonable. We must absolutely align on a common path forward that is sustainable and manageable by the leaders within these roles. Anything other than a concerted effort forward in partnership among key stakeholders will lead to conflict and disappointment.

Employee resource groups show the promise of the opportunity to help move people in various dispositions toward understanding, grace, awareness, and engagement in the greater cause of diversity, equity, inclusion, and belonging. They offer a space for individuals of similar identity to gather and build community around shared experiences and supporting one another. They also serve a very important role of informing the company of any needs, issues, and opportunities from the perspective of the group. Allies can be involved to support any initiatives that extend to the company as a whole. The potential for impact by and with employee resource groups is expansive.

This book aims to inspire ERG leaders to make a difference in their organization, no matter their role, level, or department. When strength and knowledge are cultivated among ERG leaders within organizations, they will feel empowered to make decisions and take action toward more inclusive efforts that benefit them and the company overall. The increasing movement toward inclusion, equity, and belonging via employee-driven efforts is seen vividly through the increase in ERG presence within organizations at large, as well as in the expansion of the types of ERGs that are being formed (for example, the push to have ERGs to support and represent neurodiversity within organizations).

ERGs can help create change for a more inclusive and just world and at the same time serve company interests. This book is not just a handbook or a reference guide as a how-to for ERGs (which exist in various forms). It also serves as a deeper call to action around how, with more effective ERGs, we can truly achieve transformation toward the DEI goals that we are setting out to accomplish in our organizations. ERGs are, in fact, essential for the deeper mission of diversity, equity, inclusion, and belonging to be achieved.

A grander vision at present has to do with a broader commitment to helping cultivate a more equitable society. Imagine the potential that DEI efforts supporting ERG initiatives could offer to the company and to the world as a whole. The opportunity of ERGs to be a source for the talent pipeline in itself is a winning advantage. If ERG leaders from underrepresented groups were influencers within their companies and rose higher in the ranks, there could be visibility and input into decisions that impacted their organization that would model policies and practices that could benefit all of society. From a competitive vantage point, companies have never had a greater need to tap the latent human capital in their workforce to better serve their customers and succeed in the marketplace. From an equity standpoint, the urgency to enhance employee inclusion has never been more acute. The time is now to act, cultivate change, and open up to the possibilities of employee resource groups at organizations.

TWO

TRANSFORMING ORGANIZATIONS

THE TIME IS NOW

Diversity, equity, and inclusion initiatives have been under scrutiny for decades, with numerous research studies[1] and thought pieces[2] countering the effectiveness of DEI training[3] and overall diversity efforts within organizations. There are a variety of motivators for organizational change that are ongoing and are needed. Organizations may be motivated by corporate social responsibility (CSR) in communicating their involvement in these initiatives as "the right thing to do," allowing them to stay in the public's good graces. However, this single perspective is not a lasting approach in organizations. What is needed is to make a clear case for the impact that DEI and ERGs have within an organization, through a direct return on investment of effort, time, resources, and leadership attention. This is called "the business case for DEI." Perhaps effective practices conducted through an inclusive and equitable lens would lead to an increase in sales, productivity, enhanced customer service, and so on.

Efforts to create an inclusive and equitable environment require both short- and long-term goals, dedicated leadership, and decision-making that reduces harm to those who are from nondominant identities.[4] The stressors of the work environment and the challenges of the society at large call into question the hyperfocused approach of serving the business without taking care of the needs of employees in an intentional way. DEI efforts that are bolted onto existing business functions, rather than organically integrated into every part of the company, will not succeed in meeting the expectations set forth. The questioning of DEI efforts persists if the approach of one-off trainings continues without a sense of purpose, vision, or overarching strategy that holds the initiatives together.

What, then, can cultivate transformational, lasting change? The events of 2020 with the global pandemic, the tragic murder of George Floyd, and the violent acts against Asians, among other stressors, have caused an awakening within more segments of society and the business sector to pay attention to the functioning of the organization and the well-being of employees, in a more holistic and connected way.[5] This pattern is not new; incidents in organizations and society as a whole have often prompted reactions by individuals in companies to spark change. Throughout the years, there have been many instances where both public outcry and employee organizing have forced company leadership to take a stand on equity and inclusion, where they couldn't or chose not to in the past. In recent times, worldwide distress around working conditions and movements for racial equity have prompted company leadership to pay close attention and act more urgently, in response to both the needs and the demands of the public, mirrored by employees' own opinions and activism.

Many companies have been limited by stakeholders—whether CEOs, managers, or other authority figures—who were unwilling to take part in conversations and activities around DEI that could be seen as promoting division, distracting from core business goals, or overly focusing on bringing more attention to an issue that was deemed less important or not worthy of a structured approach. Grievances raised by employees may have been handled on a case-by-case basis without addressing the larger systemic issues that created an organizational environment that led to these challenges in the first place. Instead, what is recommended is to resolve issues as they arise with the mindset of preventing them in the future. This proactive approach can be supported by clear guidance and continued commitment from leadership to cultivate an inclusive organizational environment. Many times, leadership is informed by the organization's employee resource groups, to help point toward issues that are pressing and how to effectively address matters that need to be attended to with a sense of purpose and urgency.

In the case of the Black Lives Matter and Stop Asian Hate movements, there were many instances of employee resource groups stepping in to help companies determine a path forward while the world around the company faced a racial reckoning and called into question how companies were helping people. Cisco had a company-wide forum with employees after the tragic murder of George Floyd, allowing for an open discussion and dialogue about employees' reactions to sensitive issues in the news and at the company. PayPal and Northrop Grumman each hosted Asian ERG–led events open to the entire company, where I spoke, that fostered conversation about the terrible hate crimes and violent acts against Asians due to bias surrounding the COVID-19 pandemic. These events allowed employees to share their feelings and reactions to events in the news and also how they may have been affected personally and at work. The nonprofit training organization called Hollaback! delivered hundreds of trainings on bystander intervention to help individuals learn how to interrupt and address biased and discriminatory acts to keep them from occurring against certain ethnic and gender groups.

Where there has been an absence of ERGs, employees of underrepresented communities have banded together, forming coalitions of employees who have used this momentum to voice concerns that have been long-standing issues. Organizations that have existing ERGs have seen a funneling of feedback and concerted action through these resource groups as a means of addressing the current times, propelling forward DEI initiatives that may have been underfunded or had lackluster support and impact in the past. The momentum gained from these groups is inspiring and also telling of what has been needed and overlooked in the past.

At the same time, there may be subtle and verbalized expectations around what role these groups serve and what the company can deliver, which can range from needing much effort to being unrealistic. This book asks and offers answers to the following questions: How can transformational change within organizations be ignited, and sustained, beyond a distinct period of time? How can DEI efforts be offered in a way that does not burden those who are already marginalized and excluded? How can we delineate the role of employee resource groups versus those of a DEI committee, human resources, and also company leaders? That is the work we have ahead and the subjects we will move through in this book. The common denominator—as an answer to all of these questions—is through the power of people.

THE SOURCES FOR TRANSFORMATIONAL ORGANIZATIONAL CHANGE

Many company leaders have shared with me how their hands have previously been tied in addressing DEI issues in a deep way because of organizational inertia and a lack of urgency for change. But the new and widespread attention created in parallel with these societal moments has allowed for a deeper conversation and for more intentional activities to take place. Executive after executive has shared the struggles they have had with moving the company forward with DEI when not all stakeholders were on the same page. At the same time, many employees at organizations have individually and collectively expressed frustration at the lack of progress that has been shown in their organizations over time. Indeed, the degree to which DEI efforts are taken seriously has reached a tipping point, by all roles within an organization. It is something that can no longer be ignored or put on the back burner. In this time of widespread concern about inclusion and equity, I have personally witnessed the upsetting power dynamics within boards of organizations and the unsettling of other influential groups, who are usually resistant to activities around DEI, due to reasons of caution and focus for the business. We have all also observed employee resource groups stepping up and rescuing organizations where there has been a lack of intentional diversity, equity, and inclusion strategy, or limited expertise on pertinent issues. The current times have brought these serious gaps to the surface.

Societal flashpoints and social movements have been a catalyst for change within companies and have proven out my model of organizational transformation, which I call the Trifecta of Organizational Change™ (see figure 3). This model outlines the components needed to press DEI issues forward, which involves the co-partnership of leadership, employees, and the public. Each of these three stakeholders has a role in organizational transformation. In recent years, events and campaigns such as the Google walkout, #DeleteUber, the Wayfair employee coalition, and the Activision Blizzard walkout have been powerful examples of how public sentiment and employee action can compel company leadership to tackle issues of inclusion and fairness.

Let's take the case of Uber as an example. I was working for a company providing consulting for a summit and training for employee resource group members at Uber in early 2017. That year, a number of key issues in the news and within the company made a drastic shift necessary. First, the ride-sharing service faced public backlash from the social media movement #DeleteUber,[6] due to accusations of price gouging during a taxi workers' strike; this transpired in the midst of protests against the presidential ban on travel to the United States by refugees and visitors from certain countries. Second, a blog post published by former Uber employee Susan Fowler detailing the sexual harassment she had faced at the company became a watershed moment for the entire organization.[7] Employee morale worsened as news continued to report more incidents that called into question the ethics of the company's operations and leadership. As a result of this push from the public and employees, Uber's leadership turned to implementing "listening sessions" to take in feedback from employees at the company. Uber's womens' ERG and Black employees' ERG rose to the forefront to articulate issues of marginalization, exclusion, and poor treatment at work. They became a conduit for raw and authentic feedback, which eventually turned the company toward more effective leadership, and it was able to regain its standing in the public.

Bernard Coleman, who at the time was Uber's Global Head of Diversity and Inclusion, shared the story of Uber's journey through this difficult time. At the 2018 annual conference hosted by the Forum on Workplace Inclusion, Coleman spoke on a panel titled "What We Do Next Matters Most: Case Studies of Crisis, Resilience, Inclusion, and Belonging at Uber and Unilever."[8] He shared how Uber implemented 100 listening sessions with the staff in conjunction with employee resource groups, "to make sure everyone had a voice in the process" and to help leadership understand "what do we need to do, where should we be going." He described how the focus was to understand, "What can we do to use the voices of the staff to improve Uber and make the company what we know it should be and can be?" Themes that came up in the listening sessions were that "diversity and inclusion is important" and that the performance review process, pay equity, and employee morale and belonging needed to be improved.

Coleman described how during this period an internal company ERG summit became a key event, where the company "really came together and talked about what was going on." He observed how the first global ERG summit relied upon the participation, feedback, and engagement of ERGs in its development and formation. He shared how Uber "pressure-tested a workshop called 'why diversity matters,' which was a live, nonmandatory workshop that almost four thousand attended," and the importance of addressing intersectionality. He talked about how the employee resource group growth had skyrocketed, describing how "we were stronger together coming out of that." He explained how employee resource groups "became culture carriers of the company" and how he tended to "rely upon them for inspiration and things that we can do." Engaging ERGs also helped with employee morale at Uber. Coleman shared how the feeling was "Together we can do this" and how he personally experienced it: "I felt I had an army of people all around the company; we were all working in concert, trying to make it what we knew it could be. It was transformational.

"Our employee resource groups . . . rallied and helped the company during a very tough, what I call, inflection moment in our company's life, and I think it helped turn the corner in doing the best and the brightest things and the most innovative things, coming from the voices from our employees. It was remarkable."

Coleman's words about ERGs and the actions created as a result of input from ERGs bring the message home about how employee resource groups can be invaluable to organizations. As he describes, ERGs are "powerful influencers in the company." This example demonstrates my Trifecta of Organizational Change™ model, which illustrates how deep organizational change can take place with the participation of key stakeholders, including leadership, employees, and the public (see figure 3). Often, the employees who gather in the form of employee resource groups can help the points of the triangle gain momentum for movement to occur.

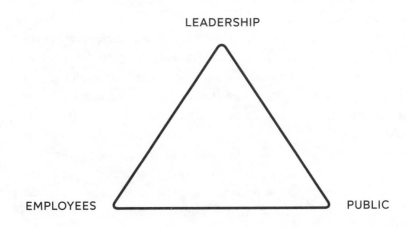

FIGURE 3. *THE TRIFECTA OF ORGANIZATIONAL CHANGE*™.

As the model demonstrates, there needs to be at least two or ideally three points of the triangle engaged in order for transformative organizational change around diversity, equity, and inclusion initiatives to take hold and start to turn. Picture the triangle spinning quickly when there is enough weight on each point. If only one point has weight, the triangle will not budge. If two points have weight, there can be some movement, but the triangle will not turn quickly. Real movement within organizations requires all three points to be engaged and to have pressure to oscillate. Otherwise, disparate activities and attempts at DEI work stay siloed and stagnant. In many cases with organizations, leadership could make some efforts that don't take hold or are seen as performative and not believable by the public—or the employees. There could also be some feedback from employees (for example, an HR complaint) that is addressed individually but not at a systemic level.

The final part of the triangle that gets an organization to move is the response from the public. Reactions from the public on social media and campaigns such as @pullupforchange, founded by Sharon Chuter, hold organizations accountable in a vulnerably transparent way. When companies are called out for the lack of diversity on their board and leadership, or for their statements addressing national issues without action or follow-up, the public immediately addresses it through social media or in news coverage. This fans the flames of unrest among employees in organizations that already are experiencing issues around a lack of DEI. As each point of the triangle receives weight and pressure, it makes the greater effort move.

If all three points of the triangle are engaged in a purposeful and intentional way, the organization can move forward at a measured pace. However, events and sudden pressures such as lawsuits, public outcry, or societal tragedy can make the company spin out of control. This creates a need for urgent responses from leadership rather than a measured approach. The peaking of issues to the point where the workplace environment is hostile—possibly prompting a walkout, lawsuit, or collective coming together of employees against leadership—is an outcome that can happen to organizations without the proper communication channels and relationships built that promote a sense of trust, accountability, transparency, and partnership. An intentional strategy can lead to long-term, transformational change toward cultivating inclusion and belonging in the workplace.

What about your organization? Reflect on the model and how it can apply to your own company context. How would you rate the involvement of all three groups: company leadership, your employees, and the public? Do you have employee networks or other groups that have organized around a common cause? Is your public and consumer audience weighing in on your activities with interest and requests for transparency and accountability? Is your leadership taking a proactive stance toward diversity, equity, and inclusion, or is it reactive to the responses of any other stakeholders only when it is urgent and absolutely necessary?

Organizations that have integrated and well-supported ERGs have the opportunity for ongoing feedback and communication, as well as a pipeline for leadership and new ideas. ERGs are often leveraged as focus groups and as a pathway for promotion for outstanding leaders. ERG leaders serve as ambassadors to the greater community, interacting with social causes and as conduits for contact with suppliers of diverse backgrounds. As with the case of Uber described here, all of these aspects of ERG involvement can happen at the same time, creating wide-scale impact across the organization that can completely shift the organization toward a better outcome.

It is clear how a company's success or failure can be tied to the engagement of its employees and enhanced by the presence and effective management of ERGs. This book focuses on how to manage ERGs effectively, as well as why organizations should pay close attention to these groups as a place for engagement, innovation, and belonging, and as a source of feedback and direction on tough issues.

The key to overall success of the company and that of its people is through empowering ERG leaders and stakeholders to be involved and connected in a cocreation and execution of company vision, while continuing long-term efforts toward equity and inclusion.

Without this deep collaboration, the true potential of both employees and the company will not fully be met. The company will also lose traction in the public domain when there is scrutiny of its actions or lack of action in external circles. Instead, ERGs can help companies move forward with the momentum, support, feedback, and encouragement of employees that are the hallmarks of company success around diversity, equity, and inclusion.

THREE

FORMING AND OPERATING ERGS

THE 5 PS OF EFFECTIVE FUNCTIONING

Are you in the process of forming a new ERG? Or do you already have ERGs in operation, and you're wondering how to run them effectively? Setting up and operating an ERG is no small feat, and there are a number of things you need to consider. In this chapter, I'll be sharing some models and best practices for how to run an ERG effectively and most efficiently. I will also share some of the common operational challenges that ERG and organizational leaders are confronted by. We will explore some of the current issues that ERGs face and where discussion is still unfolding, with a deeper look at contemporary issues that are surfacing in the field.

FORMING AN ERG

Are you or your organization interested in creating an ERG? Do you have enough interest from others to form a group? What support do you have from leadership? Is there a framework in place for you to launch a new network? Are you considering starting multiple ERGs? If so, which group should be started first, and what about starting others at the same time? How do you go about all of this? If you have any or all of these questions, you are not alone! ERGs are constantly being formed at organizations around the world and for many different demographics and populations.

There are several basic building blocks you need for the ERG to be successful, sustainable, and thriving. In this chapter, I will share key aspects that are recommended for forming an ERG, as well as a checklist for you and your group as you get started. If you already have an ERG in existence, it may be helpful to reflect on these points and review this list to see if you have these essential components in place. Many times, steps are skipped in the forming of ERGs, and they function just fine—and that can work for some time. However, your group may find that it runs into challenges if certain key decisions haven't been made or pertinent info is missing. As a best practice, it is important to review how the ERG is functioning each year, especially as you onboard new members and leaders, to make sure everyone is on the same page with the operations and objectives of the ERG.

As you are thinking about forming an ERG, reflect on the purpose of the ERG, as well as whom it will serve. Who would be the main members of this ERG? How will it support both the organization and the employees who are a part of the group?

As an ERG is formed, it is important to have a charter to document the founding date of the ERG, leadership positions and governance, and additional operating guidelines. In the next chapter, I delve into the different roles involved with ERGs. In this section, let's discuss the formation of an ERG, structure, guidelines, and best practices for how to operate an ERG.

STEPS FOR FORMING AN ERG

1. Establish the objective.

2. Garner interest (identify at least five to seven founding members of the ERG, including allies).

3. Establish the charter.

4. Assess stakeholder disposition.

5. Establish governance, including lines of reporting and advising, and structure for receiving feedback and approvals.

6. Utilize the 5 Ps framework introduced below for operating guidelines for your ERG.

7. Address key issues as your group develops through dialogue and careful decision-making.

The first steps for forming an employee resource group include establishing the objective of the group, and also garnering interest and gathering at least five to seven individuals (to demonstrate interest and leadership) who would be founding members. You may already know a couple of people who are interested, and you should go beyond your immediate network and invite others to also participate. After the ERG is formed, it is advisable to make a public announcement that this group is coming into existence. This ensures that the process is open to all and is equitable for those who may not be in the same circles as the individuals who are first forming the group. Note that the formation of the group may be initiated by company leadership or by a group of interested individual employees. The circumstances for forming an ERG are different for every organization.

As you begin forming your group, it's time to note key elements into what is called a *charter*. Your charter is the founding document that accounts for the formation of the employee resource group, specific guidelines around who is involved, the purpose of the group, and any operating principles that are important to note, including the role of the executive sponsor (the senior leader who will champion the ERG internally), budgetary guidelines, term limits, and requirements for communication and meetings. The charter document should be a fairly brief document that outlines the main points of the group. Any type of document outlining operating guidelines in more detail beyond those in the charter can be changed from year to year as needed. The charter is a foundational document that is not usually changed and remains in its original form over a few years. HR, DEI leads, or company leadership may have a template document that can be filled out by each employee resource group to keep the information specific and consistent. It may be helpful to get together with other ERGs that have already formed or are forming at your organization to compare notes and share ideas about what should be included in the charter document.

OPERATING AN ERG

To help support your charter and also define the operating principles of your ERG, I have developed a framework to aid in the functioning of your ERG. At its core, the role of the ERG is ultimately to serve its members and your organization at the same time. How can this be done in the most effective way? As we continue on in this chapter, we will discuss best practices for operating your ERG and also common key issues.

The 5 Ps of ERGs

There are five elements, which I call *the 5 Ps*, needed to successfully operate an ERG: (1) Purpose, (2) People, (3) Processes, (4) Planning, and (5) Priorities (see figure 4).

FIGURE 4. *THE 5 PS OF ERGS.*

PURPOSE What is the purpose of your employee resource group, if you really think about it? It is tempting to be excited to gather with other members of the same identity group at your organization, but it is important to identify the key reasons for having this employee resource group exist in a formalized way. If these reasons can be articulated in the form of a vision or mission and written down, that will serve your group in staying focused and keeping in the direction of where you want to go. Please take a moment to write down your vision and mission and share it with the rest of your ERG leaders and eventually your members. The purpose of your ERG should be clear and articulated in a way that is easy to understand for both members and your general company community. There are many people who will not be a part of the employee resource group who would like to know what is going on and its purpose. All employee resource groups should support the identities they serve. At the same time, your particular ERG may have specific reasons for existing and goals that it would like to achieve. That is why it is important to write down the vision and mission and articulate them to others. It is easy to get distracted by many opportunities and ideas that will undoubtedly form as you continue operating your ERG.

PEOPLE The people involved in employee resource groups are the core of how the group operates. Without its people, there is no employee resource group! Key stakeholders involved in the ERG range from the members themselves to the leaders, executive sponsors, a diversity council (a cross-functional group focused on diversity goals in the organization), and more stakeholders. As defining the roles and relations among each of these is so critical, I have dedicated the entire next chapter of this book to speaking about the people involved. For now, make a list of the key stakeholders involved with your group, and think about your goals for engaging each one of them.

PROCESSES Let's discuss the processes needed to effectively operate an employee resource group. The first step is to establish a regular cadence of meetings and to understand and define the reporting structure of whom the ERG shares updates with and receives approval for decisions from. There is a process for making decisions, gaining approval for budget, moving forward with events, and also communicating to the rest of the ERG and the company. What are the steps for those approvals? To whom do the ERG leaders turn for advice, approval, support, and any questions? There should be an established line of reporting and advising from the ERG to human resources leaders, DEI leaders, or another point person at the company who oversees the groups, like a community and belonging manager. This manager helps streamline processes and offers support and approvals for decision-making and budgetary requests. They are also invaluable at guiding ERGs through the dynamics of the organization and addressing any needs that arise.

In addition to reporting structure, there are other processes that need to be determined. How much money is an employee resource group allocated per year? How are budgetary requests approved?

How do you get the input of executive team members on a large company event and have them say a few opening remarks? These types of queries are common, and regular communication with the advisors to the group can be supportive of answering those questions. Having regular meetings with the HR, DEI, or community relations manager in charge of the ERGs can help answer those questions and foster a sense of confidence in ERG leaders that they are on the right track.

PLANNING Once you have the people and processes in place, it is important to plan the year's activities and even have goals for each month. First, the group should specify what meetings will occur each month and what communications will be sent out to the ERG membership. How often will communications to the ERG membership be expected? What is needed to prepare for the membership meetings each month? How often will the ERG leaders make preparations for the other activities? What types of surveys and feedback forms can be helpful to administer to the membership in order to plan events? It is important to start with feedback from the members in addition to ideas from the leadership to make sure that they are in alignment.

In addition to this, it is essential to come back to the purpose, vision, and mission of the employee resource group in the first place. If the vision is to promote career advancement of a certain demographic group within the organization, then perhaps there can be discussions around mentoring programs and other activities that can support individuals' career development and professional goals. If the objective of the ERG is to impact organizational culture to make it a more inclusive place to work, then activities that promote a sense of belonging and equity and inclusion for individuals of marginalized groups will be of utmost importance. If a goal is for the ERG to have more connections with the community or to build partnerships with associations in the industry, then perhaps there can be initiatives and subcommittees that are dedicated to this cause.

All in all, the importance of the planning phase of employee resource groups cannot be overstated. Activities such as a leadership retreat or an all-hands meeting can be used for planning and for incorporating ongoing dialogue with members and input from surveys and feedback forms. Planning can be prompted by current events and also issues that arise within the organization around the employee population that the ERG is serving. It is recommended to have some main goals and activities planned throughout the year and also to have flexibility in case urgent needs arise or an issue that is current in the news needs attention. As we have seen in the past years, there have been a number of instances when societal and global events have grabbed everyone's attention, and employee resource groups have stepped up to address the needs.

One example of this is that ERGs have been places where there have been open discussions around troubling issues and violence against marginalized communities. The need for safe spaces to disclose true feelings and support through mental health initiatives may go beyond the initial role of the employee resource group but is something that ERGs have pivoted toward becoming for their members. It is important to equip your ERG with the ability to hold space in those moments and also support it with company resources such as employee assistance programs (EAPs) that offer resources and support that go beyond what employee resource groups can provide, such as workplace wellness programs and counseling.

Often, employee resource groups are the source of feedback on whether these programs are being utilized or are sufficient and if employees know about them. It is a wonderful partnership and synergy to have employee resource groups as a vehicle for sharing important news such as access to these resources. Again, there can be plans for activities throughout the year, and at the same time there needs to be flexibility for when urgent needs arise, even in uncertain and unanticipated ways.

Common activities that are planned throughout the year for employee resource groups include social mixers, guest speakers, leadership retreats, mentoring conversations and programs, wellness and mental health workshops, community volunteering days, and more. Employee resource groups emphasize opportunities for personal and professional development and offer many resources for them. With your own group, you can plan for a calendar year of activities and aim for certain objectives to be accomplished in each quarter. This can help you vary your activities and make sure that you are covering all the aims of the members who may have different interests at the same time.

The approach I encourage is cross-collaboration across employee resource groups. This is such a phenomenal way to connect with others, preserve budgets, and show solidarity and support to others within the company across identity demographic groups. If you're planning your own group's events, make sure to check in with the leaders of other groups to see if there can be some joint events and activities that you can hold together. It also helps lighten the calendar to have events that tie in together, so that employees are not overwhelmed with having to choose between activities that may occur at the same time. This is important to consider, and having discussions and a joint strategy with other groups can be a benefit to your planning.

PRIORITIES How do you prioritize activities throughout the year? One tip is to brainstorm all the activities you'd like to do in a year and set out to organize when each of these events can take place and how they align with key moments throughout the year, such as heritage months, and also the company calendar. For example, it may be advantageous to consider inviting an African American speaker to address your company in conjunction with Juneteenth events at a celebration already planned at your organization. Or, maybe a CEO-backed initiative around work-life balance would be the perfect opportunity to have your parents' ERG partner on a joint event with the initiative and have your CEO offer opening remarks. Consider the example of a supplier diversity team that has a focus on incorporating suppliers who are veterans. Your veterans' employee resource group can ask community partners to support small business and potential vendors coming to an upcoming procurement fair planned

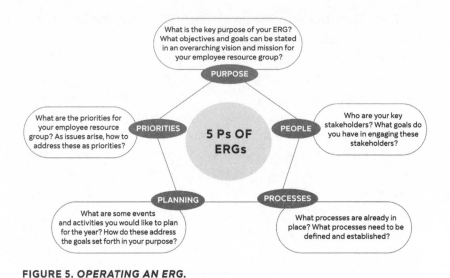

FIGURE 5. *OPERATING AN ERG.*

by your company. Planning with priorities in mind is both strategic and a way to ensure sustainability of your ERG. There are multiple avenues of interest, resources, and support that will ensure that ERG activities are relevant and impactful.

Involving the right people to help plan and prioritize your events will ensure that your activities are approached in a strategic way. That brings together the components of people, processes, planning, and priorities. These fundamentals are essential to consider when operating your ERG to maximize its success.

The 5 Ps diagram and framework can be a starting point for brainstorming and organizing with your employee resource group each year (see figure 5).

KEY ISSUES

You may be part of an employee resource group that is already in operation and has faced some key issues that are challenges in how you successfully run the group. Or perhaps as you're planning the formation of your new group, it would be interesting for you to learn about common challenges that employee resource groups face. This next section surfaces the common questions that arise around how your ERGs operate.

REWARD AND RECOGNITION

Recognizing the accomplishments of employee resource groups along the way is a fundamental part of ensuring that there is retention among ERG leaders and members, boosting morale, and showcasing the ERG's impact not only for its circle of members and participants but for the entire company overall. This recognition is important to continue because it demonstrates the value of ERGs to management and leadership so that they will support continued efforts and resources being invested in ERGs. It is also important to recognize individuals who have stood out as key leaders of the ERG. Often, a handful of ERG leaders are the driving force behind the group. In addition, there is usually a larger team of dedicated ERG leaders and members who have all put in time, attention, and effort to help initiatives launch and be successful. Recognition from top company leadership goes a long way. This can be shown in the form of a message, invitation to important events where ERG voices can be heard and their presence can make an impact, or mention at larger company or public stakeholder meetings where updates about ERGs can be shared. These forms of recognition can go a long way.

Companies with established ERGs might hold a DEI summit with an ERG component and an ERG awards and recognition dinner. Here, companies may highlight and feature top initia- tives that have been impactful throughout the year, honoring and acknowledging each ERG's efforts and contributions through a video montage or mention onstage. Any examples of larger impact to the community can be shared. ERG leaders feel recharged and motivated when their work and efforts have been recognized as a team and individually, and as a part of the larger collective of people working toward transformative change.

Additionally, it is important to recognize ERG efforts across the company so that individuals who are less involved with the efforts but manage or interact with the employees involved can get a better understanding of the work that is being done, why it is so vital to the organization, and its tremendous impact. Many times, there is a strain on the relationship between managers and employees who are involved with ERGs, because the ERG members may be seen as spending too much time on ERG initiatives from the perspective of managers, and perhaps ERG leaders feel that their managers don't understand or support them in what they are contributing to the ERG. Both perspectives are important to acknowledge. The way forward is through increased awareness about the contributions and impact of the ERGs. If there can be mutual agreement about what are reasonable expectations and efforts, as well as open sharing about the support that is needed, then ERGs can be adopted with support and integrated into organizations effectively. For many ERG members, the ease with which they can participate is a reward in itself.

Another form of reward and recognition is tied to an employee's performance review. Companies have a range of approaches in how they connect efforts within an ERG to an individual performance review. Some companies may not formally connect contributions to ERGs with an individual's performance, but that individual may have an increased visibility within a company that can lead to consideration for involvement with special projects, other roles that lead to more opportunities, and overall career advancement. I always advise ERG leaders to update their LinkedIn profiles to showcase their ERG roles and to make sure their ERG work is counted and expressed publicly.

A hot topic that has always been present but has been gaining popularity in mainstream media is whether ERG leaders should be financially compensated for their work. In fall 2020, Twitter announced that it would pay its business resource group leaders, mentioning how "this work is essential to Twitter's success—it is not a 'side hustle' or 'volunteer' activity."[1] Twitter leadership commented on how its business resource groups "are the lifeblood of inclusion efforts at Twitter."

In 2021, LinkedIn followed suit by announcing that it would pay its ERG chairs. In addition to giving its employees a paid week off "to help reduce stress and burnout," LinkedIn made an announcement that it would pay "the global co-chairs of their employee resource groups $10,000 a year."[2]

Teuila Hanson, the chief people officer at LinkedIn, stated that "historically, these employees take on leadership roles and the associated work in addition to their day jobs, putting in extra time, energy, and insight. And despite the tremendous value, visibility, and impact to the organization, this work is rarely rewarded financially."

At this writing, LinkedIn had 10 ERGs, 20 global cochairs, and more than 5,000 members and allies, and its more than 500 leaders were also to be recognized in a new nonfinancial rewards system.[3] LinkedIn expressed how there is "no price on the emotional labor and investment of time" that ERGs contribute and acknowledged that $10,000 was the first step toward wider reward for the work and a formal, systematized recognition plan.

In the case of both organizations, the initiative for compensation and recognition was in acknowledgment of how their employees were a key part of diversity, equity, and inclusion efforts but might be at the precipice of feeling burnout and not having enough resources in exchange for their efforts.

A 2021 study by the Rise Journey showed that 5.6 percent of companies surveyed paid their ERG leads.[4] They also noted that ERG leaders tend to be Black, Indigenous, and people of color (BIPOC) and other underrepresented minorities, due to the nature of the work and the identities of the individuals. What does this mean? In addition to doing extra work, and having the knowledge, passion, and commitment to contribute to the ERGs, these individuals are working *extra* to benefit the company overall, *without* added compensation.

The counter-argument could go like this: What if these individuals put as much effort into their actual work positions as they did with their "side-of-the-desk job," of being an ERG leader? What could their careers look like? Perhaps they would have career success related to their actual positions. But then the downside would be: What kind of organizational culture would they be working in? For many ERG leaders and members, there is no choice. One must contribute to the organization in this way, or the environment might lack any sense of inclusion or belonging, or even be intolerable. ERGs are a place of both community and solace, a coming together and a container for the efforts and commitment that show promise for deep, authentic experiences of equity and inclusion to take hold and be amplified.

For officers and leaders of ERGs, there can also be an array of activity levels that are different across members and leaders. One organization I was advising saw an uptick of activity from BIPOC group members after the tragic murder of George Floyd. There was a lot of discussion and attention as to how to better serve BIPOC personnel at the company, and a select group of BIPOC leaders created a document to express ideas as to how to better attract, retain, and serve BIPOC staff at the company. The ERG leaders were compensated a onetime spot bonus for the immense efforts that were offered during this particularly intense time. Although there was no ongoing compensation for ERG members and leaders, this was a good showing of effort from the organizational leadership to honor and acknowledge the efforts put forth by BIPOC employees, in particular during a time of great stress.

Given these dynamics, what are the options for employee resource group leaders being offered recognition by their companies? Companies must do an analysis of what is equitable for leaders who are carrying the charge of ERGs and decide how to support ERG leaders. ERG leaders should make sure that their commitments to the ERG don't compromise their career work and that they have support from their managers to engage in activities in a way that doesn't interfere with their existing projects.

Dalana Brand, VP People Experience and Head of Inclusion & Diversity at Twitter, summarizes the findings from company-wide listening sessions with their business resource groups (BRGs), "The most common theme was around resourcing and support: Tweeps were struggling to balance their full time role with their vast BRG responsibilities, their managers didn't have visibility into their BRG work or the tools to empower them, and there was confusion about where to go in the business for resources or support. We also heard a lot about the desire to be more globally inclusive and intersectional in the work—but they already had too much on their plate."[5] Brand describes the company's commitment to supporting BRG leaders with additional stupport, dedicated resources, new BRGs, and also formal compensation. She acknowledges that the BRG role "is not a "side-hustle" or volunteer activity."

The company also provided a statement over email, reinforcing these sentiments: "Resource group leaders not only perform their core job function, but they also commit to leading a diverse community of up to hundreds of Tweeps around the world."[6] The role of ERG leaders is vital to the overall organizational culture, DEI efforts, and leadership of communities across the organization and around the world. As such, reward and recognition for the efforts of ERG leaders should be considered with care and integrity.

Here are some tips for the conversation about determining equitable recognition and reward of employee resource group leaders. Most ERG roles at this time are voluntary, but there can be means to provide recognition and reward in other ways.

As your organization continues supporting the launch and operations of employee resource groups, the framework of the 5 Ps—Purpose, People, Processes, Planning, and Priorities—can be a useful tool for focusing the direction and approach of the ERGs. As leadership navigates how to most effectively support ERGs, key issues such as reward and recognition of ERG leaders must be considered and addressed. Continuing the conversation about supporting employee resource groups, we will next focus on a core element: their people.

....

QUESTIONS FOR REFLECTION:
FORMING AND OPERATING ERGS

1. What expectations are in the ERG charter around term limits and the commitment level of ERG leaders?

2. What is the average number of hours that the ERG leader or officer is contributing per month? What about any other ERG committee leaders?

3. How many events per month are being conducted by this ERG? What is the frequency of participation in events by each ERG leader?

4. How many ERG members are being served by this position?

5. What are some key outcomes that have been achieved through this ERG?

6. What resources are needed by the ERG?

7. What can be provided to ERG leaders as financial compensation or that is as valuable as financial compensation, such as additional vacation time or other valued benefits?

8. What other questions are important for your group to discuss, in order to define how to operate your ERG most effectively?

FOUR

THE PEOPLE BEHIND THE PURPOSE

ENGAGING ERG LEADERS, MEMBERS,
ADVISORS, AND PARTNERS

When we consider supporting ERGs, much thought and organization goes into the structure of the group. The makeup of the team and the stakeholders who are key leaders, members, and supporters are a key consideration for ERGs. In this chapter, we will go over the roles of the people who are behind much of the planning and who can influence the group to move forward. As we begin, think about the people who are involved with your employee resource group. Who are they? Who could be more engaged and also involved with the leadership and activities of the group? I will be sharing a number of different perspectives on how to activate people to be more committed, engaged, and focused in terms of their involvement with a group. Whether you are a newly formed ERG or a network that has been around for a very long time, it is prudent to reflect on the roles of individuals in your group and evaluate the strength of relationships among them.

For those of you who have been in employee resource groups for a very long time, think about new members who may not know the ins and outs of the people involved in ERGs. How can you take the information from this chapter and share it with them? How can you pass on your experience running employee resource groups to those who are new to the group? As we move through these concepts, we must acknowledge that ERG leadership is constantly in transition and that not everyone coming into a group has the same level of foundational knowledge. It is essential to go over the fundamentals of employee resource groups so that all people involved are equipped to offer their best possible contributions and support. If you're new to ERGs, welcome to this exciting new path! If ERGs are very familiar to you, think about how you can teach these critical points to others.

KEY STAKEHOLDERS

As you set up your employee resource group, be sure that you have the right leadership in place. Most ERGs start with a handful of dedicated and passionate individuals who belong to the identity of the group or are allies. These individuals become the first leaders of the ERG. They are stewards who help set the group's direction. The tone that is set with these individuals is of utmost importance and needs to be aligned with HR and company approaches to diversity, equity, and inclusion. Employee resource groups should be promoted by the company as an opportunity to be a part of an initiative and network that has endless possibilities for supporting both employees and the company. Clarity around the purpose and potential of an employee resource group can help focus participants on creating community, building a collective around the identity, and offering a safe space where there is the ability to gather and connect about issues that are common to the group's members.

There is also a need to ensure proper structural support of the group so that it can effectively navigate organizational dynamics, secure funding, and also create the biggest impact. That is where the role of the executive sponsor comes in. An executive sponsor is an individual in a top leadership position in the company who can assist the group in achieving its goals through mentorship, advising, navigating organizational dynamics, and also leveraging power, influence, and budget. Executive sponsors can be from the identity group of the ERG or of a different demographic. There are pros and cons to both. One advantage of having someone who is of the same demographic of the group is that there is a greater understanding of the group's needs, due to the common lived experience and identity of the person and the group overall. An executive sponsor who is of the same identity can also be a role model to others, especially if employees do not normally see someone of their identity in a top leadership role. In contrast, having an executive sponsor with a different identity than the ERG means they can be both an ally and an advocate, explain the needs and interests of the group to different populations in the organization, and win support for this advocacy due to their role, position, and identity. An example of this is having a male executive sponsor for a women's ERG, because he can explain and advocate for the needs of the group with his male counterparts. This is invaluable, as ERGs run the risk of becoming siloed and insulated if they keep to themselves and do not build connections with other groups.

Determining who should be an executive sponsor for your group is an important decision because they also represent connection to their function or department within the organization. That can open doors for your ERGs that are trying to build awareness and increase engagement or involvement with a particular group of the organization.

Consider the example of an Asian employee resource group I was advising. One of the executive sponsors of this group was a White male business leader in charge of technology. When they shared with this IT leader examples of cultural misunderstandings and anti-Asian bias within the company through an ERG-led event, he became aware in a deep way of the experiences of many of his direct employees. As a result, he made significant changes in the onboarding of new managers who were to work with staff of Asian background. He made sure that training for new managers in his department included education around Asian communication and behavioral norms to improve collaboration and overall team performance in his department. I heard feedback from the Asian employee resource group leaders that this was a direct result of the event hosted by the ERG and that it positively impacted company functioning. In the case of disability-focused ERGs, it is important to hear the stories of leaders who have navigated through the company to model being open about disability and the needs that can be met through dialogue and awareness. It may be inspiring for members of the employee resource group to see that modeled in their executive sponsor relationship. As we can see, there are a number of reasons for choosing an executive sponsor of the same identity as the employee resource group or a sponsor of a different identity. This is important to consider as you engage the leader who will help guide the group.

Ideally, executive sponsors should be both champions and connectors. They should be able to use their power and influence to open doors and find solutions for when the employee resource group leaders get stuck. They also can be the conduit to overall company leadership to help guide executives and senior leaders in understanding the needs and potential of the ERGs. Having a strategically positioned executive sponsor who has an ear to the ground with the employee resource group and also has access and positionality to be in regular contact with senior leaders is a tremendous benefit.

A way to maintain good relations and communication with the executive sponsor is to schedule regular meetings between the executive sponsor and the chairs of the employee resource group so that the sponsor receives ERG updates and feedback on the group's progress. An executive sponsor who does not know what is going on cannot be there to help the ERG in its time of need. Senior leadership and executive teams also appreciate the input from the executive sponsor, so that they can plan accordingly and align business goals with the workings of the ERG. This is essential for the group's sustainability and ongoing support through investment of time, resources, and funds in the group.

As the charter of the employee resource group dictates, there are usually leaders who are in charge of overall functioning and decision- making. Usually there is one or more chairs, as well as others who are in charge of portfolios such as finance, taking minutes, and membership engagement. These roles can have titles such as treasurer or membership relations lead, among others. What is important is to determine the leaders for each of these roles and set clear expectations around tasks and responsibilities, anticipated communication with executive sponsors and other company leaders, attendance at events, and presence at meetings. In practice, work duties may limit the ability of resource group leaders to attend every event and meeting, but having a clear direction and understanding is important for reducing any miscommunication or conflict.

The ERG's charter also outlines term limits. It is important to limit the terms of the group leaders so that they don't burn out and also to allow planning for new leaders to take on the roles at some point. This succession planning is essential for the long-term functioning of the group, so that the growth, development, and skills that are gained within the position can be experienced by more than just a few people at a time. Having committees to focus on certain aspects of the ERG is a good way to help develop a pipeline of leadership candidates, helping people become ready to take on officer roles within the group.

Of course, your members are a key part of your employee resource group! How do you reach your members, and how do you keep them engaged once they are a part of your group? There are some challenges with identifying who should join your group because you legally cannot target individuals in the company based on their last name, appearance, or other identifying characteristics. So the first communication to solicit participation in your group has to be sent to the entire organization. After that, individuals may elect to join your mailing list and can be contacted directly. Anyone can join an employee resource group, as it must be open to all members of your organization, regardless of identity. Your ERG may have members of the targeted demographic alongside allies and friends. Additionally, there are people who may belong to more than one affinity group at the same time. It is important to honor and acknowledge the intersectionality of identity and the multifaceted backgrounds that can be found at your organization.

The way to acknowledge, recognize, and fully include individuals of multiple backgrounds is to make sure that your communications are inclusive of all people and uplift the identity that you are wanting to focus on. An example of this for a Black affinity group would be to make sure that communications include people of multiracial backgrounds and transracial adoptees, who may not feel that they belong in the group due to their upbringing, appearance, or cultural background. This is essential for enabling true inclusion even within the specific demographic groups.

Although there is definitely a need for conversation around the different aspects of a given identity, the crucial place to start is with inclusion and welcoming of everyone into the group, in order to set the foundation for more complex conversations. For example, if someone is Latinx and also identifies as part of the lesbian, gay, bisexual, transgender, queer, intersex, asexual (LGBTQIA+) community, make a point to plan events and meetings that don't overlap, so this individual can participate fully in both groups at the same time. Another ideal option is to hold joint events, so that individuals who identify with more than one group can feel a sense of belonging and coming together around these identities. This honors the intersectionality of individuals at the organization and creates a deeper conversation, understanding, and awareness of the multifaceted nature of our personal and communal identities.

We must recognize that there are members of certain demographic groups who don't feel comfortable belonging to the ERG and may opt to join other ones. I recall speaking at a utility company's diversity summit, which was specifically aimed at supporting the company's employee resource groups. A member of the Black employee resource group asked, "What do we do about Black coworkers who don't want to join our employee resource group? How do we get them involved?" That individual remarked that they noticed people were more likely to join the "emerging professionals" resource group and other intergenerational and professional groups rather than the Black employee resource group. This was an excellent point, and it spoke to a phenomenon that can be found across many different demographics. A key reminder about employee resource groups is that these are completely optional, and people can choose to participate and attend as they wish.

People choose not to participate in an employee resource group for various reasons. They have their own identity journey, and there are dynamics, politics, and questions of safety for a member of a marginalized group within an organization that has a different dominant culture. Someone may not join an ERG because they feel less connected with that part of their identity, or perhaps they feel more interested in the other parts of their identity and want to explore those more. Or perhaps they have felt judged in the past—at previous workplaces, at home, at school, or in faith communities—and don't want to be subjected to that judgment by others at work. All of those reasons are opportunities for employee resource groups to focus on becoming more welcoming and offering a safe space for people to participate of their own will and accord. A tactical way to support people who may feel this way could be to partner on events and allow for some cross-collaboration across employee resource groups, to demonstrate the impact and direction of the ERG to the entire company.

You may also encounter people who are ashamed of their identity, due to how they grew up or what their parents and society taught them about pride in their identity. This is a sensitive topic, and there should be no judgment around whether someone is fit to be part of a group. Employee resource groups and affinity groups could be places that allow members to reconnect to their identity and provide a sense of true belonging that can help heal shame, pain, and marginalization around the identity that may have resulted from previously being excluded or judged. For some people, it could also be a question of safety in the workplace. For example, you may know that someone has a same-sex partner but is not part of the Pride group. That is their own personal choice, and it could be related to their experiences of being out in public or not. Again, there should be some caution and sensitivity around the involvement of individuals and allowing that to be a choice for the prospective employee resource group members themselves. The bottom line is to be welcoming and to offer a space for people to participate when they are ready. It is of absolute importance to reduce potential harm and retraumatizing of individuals who may already feel triggered or have a sense of alarm due to their identity and experiences of marginalization.

That being said, it is completely understandable that there is eagerness around involving more employees in your group! As your group gains momentum and visibility, its presence and what it stands for will be more accepted and understood by everyone at the company and by individuals of the identity demographic themselves. As ERG members and leaders serve as role models to others, and as members of the group share their own stories and journeys, people will feel more at ease with honoring that part of who they are.

We have talked about the leaders of the employee resource group, the executive sponsor, and also the group's members. Who are other stakeholders that could be involved in the equation? Your organization may have a larger diversity council that helps guide the organization's efforts with respect to diversity, equity, and inclusion. There should be clarification as to where employee resource groups fit with the diversity council. Do the executive sponsors sit on this council or report to it? Do your HR leaders share updates from the employee resource groups with this council? As your organization defines the structure and lines of reporting, think about the position of the employee resource group and whom it needs to communicate with. Perhaps the ERG chairs directly share updates with the diversity council once every six months. Or there could be a larger, company-wide diversity summit where ERGs share an update.

One organization I was consulting to offered a midyear company-wide diversity summit where the employee resource group leaders were invited to share updates on the progress of their groups as well as any questions they had for leadership moving forward. This was a powerful catalyst for conversation among the entire company, and it allowed the employee resource groups to shine in all that they had achieved, accomplished, and organized throughout the year. It also helped those who were not a part of the affinity groups to hear what the groups were doing and to have a deeper understanding of the impact that the ERGs were having on organizational culture and belonging for employees. Additionally, it helped with creating alignment around a DEI strategy by the diversity council leaders and communicating how the employee resource groups are a key part of DEI at the company.

Another group of stakeholders to remember is the other employee resource groups! They are your biggest allies, advocates, and companions in this process. They may be going through what you were going through, in a similar way or a different way. It is best to maintain relations with other ERGs in order to share resources and also offer support through common challenges that may be faced by each group. Many leaders find it beneficial to develop relationships and cross-collaboration among employee resource groups through joint activities, annual general meetings, shared speakers, and other means of interacting as a show of support and solidarity. Planning events together is advisable, as it helps save on the budget needed to conduct activities and allows ERGs to share expenses.

Employee resource groups might be encouraged by the company to submit a budget for their activities and plans for the year. This may be a requirement for each ERG separately, and there could be a feeling of competition around who gets the most budget funds and approval for activities from HR and senior leadership. It is best to avoid any sense of competition and instead support each other and the different ERGs in the company. I witnessed an allyship-based ERG offer some of their allocated budget to a BIPOC employee resource group, on top of their already allocated funds, in a tremendous show of support. This joint plan was fostered by HR in the company as well as the ERG leaders and executive sponsors. In this case, it would have been easy to split the budget down the middle, but this shows how there was an ongoing sense of collaboration, allyship, and open communication among these ERGs.

Other stakeholders to be mindful of could be the public, community partners, the press, and other groups that may interact with your employee resource group. How can you best leverage and engage with these partners? Are there communications or meetings that need to take place in order to establish and continue building a relationship with these stakeholders? Keep these groups in mind as a part of your plan. Continuing the relationship can take place in a number of ways. The key is not only to reach out when the ERG needs something, but also to offer invitations to attend events, joint education, or other activities that could be of value to the other partner. Employee resource groups could offer access to conferences and free passes to events that the general community would normally not have access to, through their partnering relationships with community organizations. This approach serves one of the pillars of employee resource groups around career advancement because it encourages a relationship that is organic and can lead to a pipeline of individuals who may be interested in working at the company in the future. The talent and career pathway created between the ERG and the greater community can be a chance to enter an industry or company that people normally wouldn't have access to.

Another example is an environmental nonprofit agency that had done a lot of work with communities of color and were advocates for relieving economic and environmental disparity in underserved neighborhoods. When questions came from the public around a push for connection and support for communities of color—with which the environmental organization had a long-standing relationship—they were able to put out a joint statement in solidarity for racial justice and also were able to showcase previous examples of partnership to this cause. Going back to our pillars of employee resource groups, this supports community building and creates positive brand visibility in the public.

You may be wondering, what if there are organizational functions that already deal with some of the stakeholder groups that you are also involved with? For example, you may have a community social responsibility or philanthropic part of your organization that deals with community partners. How can you best engage with community partners directly, if these departments are also involved? The key here is to have open communication and transparency around who is in the best position for the relationship and also whose responsibility that relationship falls under. For example, if there are donations to be made to a community-based organization around domestic violence, and if you have an employee resource group on mental health, perhaps there can be a coming together of both the philanthropic part of your organization and the mental health–based employee resource group to support this ongoing relationship and charitable funding.

This is a win-win for companies, as it offers more connections across the company in different ways. Employees would be proud to be a part of initiatives that support a cause that they believe in, and the company can support the relationship building through formalized networks such as charitable giving, press releases, and opportunities to have joint events in celebration of these partnerships. There could be an introduction that could start with the employee resource group and then be handed off to the corporate social responsibility or public affairs parts of the organization.

Just as any employee would normally speak to your communications department about any press materials that would go out, employee resource groups should foster relationships with different departments to help the ongoing activities they are a part of as they work with community and public stakeholders.

In the same way, if there are any innovative ideas around marketing or product development that would penetrate other functions of the business, they should be received as valuable forms of input. One way to help with receiving that input, without its being challenging to the organization of functions, is to develop a process and feedback loop where some of that information can be shared with the organization in a formalized way. The executive sponsor and the ERG chairs would be involved with how to give that feedback appropriately to each department. Nationally, senior leaders should be clear that employee resource groups are a priority and that they offer valuable insights that represent perspectives from the public that normally would not be heard or seen in the functions of an organization with a particular dominant culture that is different from these underrepresented groups. There need to be clear directives around how this input should be valued, received, and responded to, so that there can be clear lines of communication and trust among all parties. If these processes are not set up, there could be an issue around questions of territory and overstepping by employee resource groups into the functions of the business. We wish to avoid any miscommunication around this. Being proactive can be a big boost to the companies seeking this type of specific feedback.

What are some other pain points that you face in operating your employee resource group? Do you find that some people are doing most of the work and others are observing but are not as involved? Do you see that there are some activities you do successfully, but you are looking for new ideas to reach out to members within your group? Do you find that your membership list is very large, but not many people come to events in person? These are all very common issues to do with the functioning and engagement of people in the group. How do you consider the main areas of development and key challenges that you face at your employee resource group, and how do you focus on which stakeholders are involved and what their needs and perspectives could be in the situation? Perhaps they are looking to engage in a way that your group doesn't already have as a formalized process. Or they could be challenged with the balance of home and work life, as well as constraints of time and competing responsibilities. As you think about the individuals who are a part of the employee resource group or who could be more involved, one very common issue is how to find time to work on ERG activities and not compromise regular work responsibilities.

How do we address the valid concern company managers have, that employee resource group leaders and members may be spending too much time on their ERG work and not enough time on their work responsibilities? This dynamic calls into question the greater functioning of ERGs within the organization and if there needs to be more communication, awareness, and buy-in through dialogue at the senior leadership and management levels, in addition to ERG leaders and members advocating for themselves. If there is a clear connection between DEI strategy, ERG activities, and ERG leaders' work within their official company role, then management can feel more assured in allowing for the release of time and focused attention to the employee resource group responsibilities, without it damaging the expectations around work.

However, in addition to ensuring that management is on board, there is the actual tactical execution of ERG activities that may compete with work. How does one balance the competing responsibilities of employee resource groups and one's role at the company? There needs to be a clear assignment and division of responsibility across leaders and members of the ERG so that one person isn't carrying the entire load. There also should be more formalized processes around DEI and HR assistance that can lend extra support so that ERG leaders can thrive and succeed at their ERG responsibilities as well as their work responsibilities.

Practically, that may mean a release of time or putting the ERG work on their performance review as an actual responsibility and part of their role. Not many organizations have this formalized process in place as ERGs are being launched. So there needs to be an open dialogue and understanding around the potential issues that can come up as employee resource groups are forming, growing, and commanding more attention and effort.

Additionally, there needs to be a sense of healthy boundaries around what is your ERG work, which should be DEI and HR work, and also what is absolutely not possible within the realm of the organization. There are a lot of movements and activities around social and racial justice, for example, that are quite labor-intensive and require much effort and attention. At some point, ERG leaders must draw a line of not taking on those added responsibilities and also be patient that the urgency around an issue will be managed as is possible within the organization.

At the same time, companies need to demonstrate taking on responsibility through their leadership and HR efforts to take charge of situations that are in the domain of company leadership and should not be in the portfolio of employee resource groups. For example, any type of company-wide initiative in efforts to address a social issue can be done through the corporate social responsibility arm of a company, in discussion with the board of directors, CEO, and senior executive leaders. Of course, we want to involve the identity demographic groups of the employee resource groups to give input on such key issues, but the burden of responsibility should not be on the employee resource groups to lead this out proactively. There is a lot of responsibility put on ERGs by themselves, and leaders of a company, to fill a role that really should be played by others.

The question remains: What if the senior leadership, HR, or other formalized body within the company does not have the knowledge or lived experience to advise on a particular issue related to an identity group? That is where there needs to be a mirror and a microscope in examining the diversity representation within a company's organizational functioning. If there is a gap in knowledge, skills, awareness, and wherewithal to bring forth an issue and address it completely, then that speaks to a larger problem in terms of an organization's capacity to effectively address issues of equity and inclusion. Again, ERG leaders who may feel called to step into these conversations need to be mindful of taking on too much responsibility. I have witnessed far too many ERG leaders doing more than they should in a situation. Although it may feel as though there is no other way but to address it or it won't get done, it really again is a statement on the need for companies to address the issue themselves.

These experiences represent symptoms of systemic marginalization of individuals and the privileges of certain individuals from dominant identities that leave companies without the expertise that is needed in this time. Unfortunately, companies have been built with remnants of established bias and norms that, over time, replicate and create environments that are not fully diverse and representative of the general population. Given that phenomenon, leaders in an organization should be mindful of overutilizing employee resource groups as the sole source for knowledge, skills, and capabilities that are lacking in the leadership team, in lieu of making deliberate commitments to increase diversity and representation at all levels of the workforce.

Finally, how does senior leadership fit into working with employee resource groups? ERGs are a source of information about employee satisfaction and experience, the public and communities they represent, and aspects of the business that may not normally be considered from the vantage point of senior leaders. As a result, ERGs are a great source of innovative thinking, feedback, and also getting a sense of the pulse of the organization in an immediate way. I highly recommend that senior leaders speak with ERG leaders regularly, in addition to their direct reports. There are many executive leaders who understand the gold mine of information that ERGs offer as a resource and opportunity for the company. It is important to establish a relationship and develop dialogue so that the relationship with ERGs not only can positively shape the company but also can elicit valuable input from senior leaders.

This close relationship is important to foster early on. Choosing an executive sponsor who can help facilitate this ongoing dialogue will help align ERG and company goals. Perhaps a business unit leader wants to learn more about the Gen Z market. It would make sense for that leader to either be an executive sponsor of the emerging professionals group or be in contact with the executive sponsor of that group to gain insights into this market. Gen Z members of a company may also be excited to offer input on certain products and service offerings that can be developed to be more tailored to the experience of Gen Z and millennial customers. This is a great method of engaging employees and fostering a deeper experience of connection between products and services at work and the people who are a part of the organization.

NETWORK MAPPING

In this chapter, we have covered the main stakeholders within employee resource groups. We talked about ERG leaders, members, executive sponsors, a diversity council, and other stakeholders, such as the public, community partners, and the press. As you reflect on your own employee resource group, consider where some of these relationships could be strengthened. Also consider which of these stakeholder groups you have strong connections with that you can leverage even further.

One method of ascertaining the strength of a relationship among your key stakeholders is to go through the exercise of network mapping. Network mapping is a wonderful way to identify the different people who are part of a group and others who may be connected to the resource group but outside of it, and reflect on whether the relationships are established, absent, or negative, or need to be strengthened. In this visual mapping exercise, write down the name of your ERG in the middle of a piece of paper. Draw lines from your employee resource group to stakeholders, and draw circles around those stakeholders. Next, draw a dotted line for where there is a relationship that could be improved, draw bold lines for relationships that are strong, draw jagged lines for relationships that are negative, and draw no line for relationships that are nonexistent. What do you notice about your own map? Which relationships are flourishing, and which areas are in need of attention and support?

As an employee resource group, reflect on where you'd like to focus on strengthening and furthering relationships. As you consider the different stakeholders that are part of your group, it is recommended to go through this exercise from time to time and acknowledge where there may be a need for more focused attention. It could also be useful to do the same exercise within your group to determine if there needs to be stronger communication among certain committees, between your officers, with your members, and even as a way to start succession planning with individuals' names in your chart. This intentional reflection on key stakeholders within and around your group can help you focus and plan what your programmatic activities need to focus on in the coming months.

The relationships you build within your own employee resource group and with other ERGs are pivotal to the sustainability and success of your ERG. People are the power behind employee resource groups, and relationships with your members, leaders, and partners are going to be the tools for success and creating lasting impact with your ERG. At the same time, employee resource groups are always in a state of transition and change. Given that, we should consistently focus on the people involved in the ERGs, continue building partnerships and collaboration, and pass on the institutional knowledge about how ERGs are run effectively to the next generation. This is what makes efforts in support of employee resource groups so meaningful and impactful. ERGs are not only networks of people within an organization but living organisms that need tending in order to grow, thrive, and positively impact their people, organizations, and communities.

FIVE

CREATING ORGANIZATIONAL IMPACT

BUILDING IN PILLARS, DRIVERS, AND METRICS FOR ERGS

Many groups form around certain affinity and identity demographics, with the excitement and intention of community building and being a support to one another. The celebration and delight resulting from seeing other faces and community members from your own identity group is indescribable. The sense of belonging that comes from employee resource groups is unparalleled at organizations. Employee resource groups and affinity groups offer a space for belonging, support, understanding, and healing that can better equip communities of marginalized identities to navigate organizational dynamics.

For those who are members of the identity group, the meaning and purpose behind employee resource groups is clear. It is to gather together with others of the same group to participate in community building and to experience camaraderie. However, there needs to be alignment with organizational objectives in order to ensure the sustainability of the ERGs and the understanding of them as a part of the organizational context.[1] This may not be as daunting or challenging a task as it may seem at first. There can be complete alignment among the affinity group and employee resource group objectives and organizational objectives. In fact, this is an imperative. There is much debate as to whether affinity groups and ERGs are simply there to celebrate "food, fun, and flags" without a deeper connection to the business.

Other parts of the organization may feel that the efforts are limited and bring value only to the members who are a part of them. This could not be further from the truth. In actuality, employee resource groups hold the potential for transforming organizations to maximize processes and practices ranging from career development, community engagement, and public relations to product testing, supplier diversity cultivation, and marketplace reach. Jennifer Brown's paper "Employee Resource Groups That Drive Business" outlines key business impact areas that ERGs can strive toward.[2] These include recruitment and retention, community outreach, professional development, HR policy, marketing to employees, marketing to customers, government relations, cultural assimilation, product development, and global development. This list contains just some of the many business impact areas that are top of mind for companies.

Employee resource groups can be quite strategic in offering benefits to many parts of the business in addition to supporting the identity group members themselves. The key here is establishing a framework where objectives can be articulated, organized, and implemented with more than one goal in mind. It is an opportunity for both employees and the business to benefit at the same time.

In this chapter, we will explore a framework I have created called "ERG Pillars," which addresses how key organizational objectives align with supporting the demographics of the affinity groups (see figure 6). For those of you who have business resource groups, business objectives may be more clearly expressed and communicated as a goal and value proposition of each employee resource group. For those of you who have resource groups and networks focused on affinity space building and community gathering, it is your opportunity to draw the connection to organizational objectives and strengthen the case for resource groups at your organization. As we dive into the pillars of ERGs, reflect on where your organization has focus and strength, and also which areas could benefit from attention and effort.

ERG PILLARS

WORKFORCE	WORKPLACE	MARKETPLACE	COMMUNITY	SUPPLIERS
Employees and leaders	Working environment	Customers and prospects	External individuals and organizations	Vendors and contractors

FIGURE 6. *ERG PILLARS.*

QUESTIONS FOR REFLECTION: ERG PILLARS

Workforce: How can ERGs attract, support, and retain the workforce? How can organizations support the workforce represented in ERGs?

Workplace: How can ERGs contribute to an inclusive workplace culture? How can organizations create a more inclusive culture for identities represented in ERGs?

Marketplace: How can ERGs offer market insights, connect with consumers and potential customers, and extend market reach? How can organizations receive input and tailor products and services to serve the communities associated with ERGs?

Community: How can ERGs align with social causes as well as connect with and give back to the community? How can organizations' corporate social responsibility and public affairs initiatives be mindful of and in alignment with the relationships, connections, and direction established by the ERGs?

Suppliers: How can ERGs help develop relationships with vendors and enhance supplier diversity? How can companies incorporate more supplier diversity, representing communities associated with the ERGs?

Workforce

The workforce pillar of employee resource groups focuses on career advancement, retention, and promotional pathways for existing employees, as well as on recruitment and hiring of new employees. In the competition for talent, ERGs help make the organization stand apart from other workplaces as an employer of choice. For new employees and potential candidates, the presence of ERGs indicates the consciousness around diversity, equity, and inclusion and a concerted effort toward belonging for employees. It also can be seen as a benefit to employees who are considering working at the organization as a place to connect with new colleagues, foster friendships, and build networks across the organization.

One ERG member shares their experience: "Prior to being active in my ERG, I was disengaged at work and frequently considered leaving my company. I never felt I fit in or that I would be able to succeed while still being my authentic self at work. Once I found my ERG, I found community. That community gave me confidence to be my authentic self and motivated me to become active in the group to ensure that everyone at my company who may be feeling the way I felt could have the opportunity to gain the trust and support I did."

Another ERG member states, "I have individually benefited from participating in my ERG because I'm an engaged employee, and I tend to read the ERG newsletters and attend events hosted by other ERGs—not just my ERG that I lead. I've probably had more opportunities to attend courses on personal branding, career advancement, social justice and equity, sustainability, and corporate responsibility than most employees. If I see something that interests me, I will attend it and learn something new. I feel like as a result, I've been exposed to different thoughts and viewpoints. This comes out in my ERG leadership, as well as my volunteerism outside of work."

These are such poignant examples of how participating in ERGs has rewarded employees through personal growth and also has increased their own engagement within their companies.

I've heard countless other stories about how employee resource groups supported individuals who were starting in a new organization or moving to a new region for the job, helping them get the lay of the land within the organization and also the neighborhood they lived in. For certain community groups, knowing where you can get your hair done or find certain foods can make for an easier integration into the new workplace culture and the region where the organization is located.

For existing employees who are a part of the employee resource group, the group offers a chance to build capacity and skills through leadership development of their ERG and exposure to project management and public speaking, in a low-risk way—such as through planning and speaking at ERG events. It also offers exposure to other parts of the business—for example, through contact with members who may work in different departments. That creates a grounded sense of connection among employee resource group members and the opportunity for career growth as well as lateral movement. All of this helps with retention of employees as they weigh external career prospects versus growth opportunities within the organization, if they stay. Additionally, hiring leaders can look to ERGs as a place where they can find talent to fill emerging roles for higher-level positions. There are many examples of senior leaders advancing within a company via employee resource group contact and involvement.

In this way, employee resource groups offer a strong value proposition for career advancement, recruitment, retention, and networking. As you reflect on your own employee resource group and organization, what are the opportunities that you offer to help foster leadership development and growth of your ERG leaders and members? What career and mentoring opportunities are available to employee resource group leaders and members? How are your senior managers, executives, and human resources professionals leaning on the network of employee resource group leaders as an avenue to fulfill roles and projects? Take a moment to intentionally plan events and activities that benefit this pillar of ERG functioning: the workforce.

Workplace

The second pillar powering your employee resource group is the workplace. Cultivating an inclusive organizational culture and equitable workplace environment is a top priority for organizations today. Much of the work from DEI efforts centers equity, inclusion, and belonging. Employee resource groups serve this pillar through many of the activities that they plan, and they can support larger strategic efforts around impacting organizational culture in a more formal way. An example of this is a financial institution that wanted to roll out diversity, equity, and inclusion training around identity, privilege, and intersectionality, in order to support a healthier workplace culture and also better serve customers. The leaders in charge of learning and development launched the initiative with the employee resource groups first to build momentum and spread the word about the importance of this training program. As a result, the company achieved significant success in terms of awareness, engagement, and participation in the program.

Overall, the employee resource groups supported enterprise-wide DEI efforts that impacted the workplace and delivery of services to customers. An ERG member mentions the impact that their ERG has had with regard to "HR policies, gender neutral toilets in the workplace, networking opportunities, creating safe space for people at the stage of coming out, and offering support for parents of LGBTQIA+ kids." These examples demonstrate the powerful impact an ERG can have on increasing understanding, awareness, and advocacy for an inclusive workplace culture for LGBTQIA+ employees and their families.

Marketplace

As we can see in exploring these pillars, many of them overlap. If we think about the previous example and how it impacted the workplace environment as well as potential customers, the marketplace pillar is another prime focus for employee resource groups. ERGs have been responsible for developing new products, helping companies understand potential consumers, and making sure that services are delivered in a culturally sensitive and appropriate way. When you think about how to reach customers, do your products and services engage consumers in the mode of communication that they prefer? Are the flavors that you have created ones that consumers of various ethnic groups would buy? Do you have any language translations of your marketing materials that incorporate regional colloquial sayings? Companies can leverage employee resource groups to support outreach and connection with consumers to win marketplace share.

Engaging employee resource groups can help manage missteps that can happen if your go-to-market strategy does not take diversity into account. For instance, a financial institution decided to put up a billboard in a primarily Korean neighborhood in Southern California. This billboard was meant to evoke "SoCal" (Southern California) culture while appealing to the Korean business community at the same time. However, the marketing leads decided to place a picture of a Filipino man surfing on the billboard. This alienated audiences in the business community in the Korean area because first, it depicted the wrong Asian group, and second, it was casual in an area that was very formal and structured in its business dealings. That financial institution lost credibility from this advertising misstep. An employee resource group would have been a good place to test out potential advertising campaigns and would have been able to offer guidance to the marketing team about who and what they chose to be represented on the billboard.

A contrasting example is a mobile communications provider that partnered with the Latinx heritage group at the company to host an event where members of the community could come and try out the latest cell phone product. There were giveaways, and many people enjoyed the event and were able to interact with the phone and get excited about the newest features. This increased brand affinity among the community, and sales of the device skyrocketed within this particular demographic.

As we can see, there are many opportunities for employee resource groups to offer feedback and insights on products and campaigns, and to directly reach customers within underserved and emerging market segments. As employee resource groups plan for the year, it is critical to align goals and activities toward supporting the business within this pillar. In preparation, business leaders can start to think ahead about how to leverage the employee resource groups as well-versed focus groups and cultural informants around particular communities that they would like to reach.

Community

The pillar of community and social responsibility is receiving heightened attention, given the push for commitment to social action and accountability around practices and approaches that incorporate community causes. This pillar of employee resource groups is fundamental for engaging employees and the public at the same time. Employees from historically marginalized communities or underrepresented identities who are a part of a company that lacks direction around social causes may feel less of a sense of belonging and be less committed to the company in the long term. The pillar of community and social responsibility embodies intent and action. This can come in the form of charitable funding to nonprofit organizations, partnering with industry associations, or volunteering time and resources to important causes. Many companies donate in-kind resources as well as funds to nonprofit, mission-driven organizations. One ERG member describes the various activities they were involved with: "We partnered with a local nonprofit to host a hygiene drive for women fleeing domestic abuse and diapers for children. With some quick organizing, we were able to make a tremendous difference. Additionally, we participated in a work clothing drive for students in need at a local college, helping build their confidence for upcoming interviews." In addition to charitable contributions, we can see here how there can be a commitment of staff time for resources that a nonprofit organization needs in order to continue offering its services.

For example, there is an organization that was tracking hate crimes in a particular ethnic community. A few companies that had engineers and technological capabilities offered hands-on assistance in building out the platform to enable a more effective tracking process for these hate crimes. This is a tremendous form of capacity building within the organization that will benefit it for years to come. Many companies also offer volunteer days when employees are able to, for instance, take one day off a quarter to volunteer time at a local organization. Companies can provide a short list of approved volunteer organizations or can even offer a day off to everyone to volunteer at a single organization at the same time. These are meaningful demonstrations of support for the community that build collaboration and relationships, showing the company's long-term commitment to external stakeholders. In turn, the company may invite community members to opportunities such as career fairs and internship programs, to continue building relationships and investment into the community. Companies that focus on community building also benefit from that brand awareness and giving back to the community.

Suppliers

The final pillar of ERGs focuses on supplier diversity. Employee resource groups can build connections with diverse suppliers and share opportunities for becoming a vendor or being certified as a minority-, woman-, LGBTQIA+-, or veteran-owned enterprise. This is a way to expand the supplier diversity pipeline for institutions and corporations in a natural and long-term way. Companies can host educational events and free training programs for small businesses to go through their business boot camps or minority certification workshops. These opportunities are highly valued by community members and directly support the development of diverse suppliers that can end up doing business with the sponsor company. It also helps with brand visibility to put on these programs and initiatives and team with employee resource groups to promote them, so that suppliers know that the opportunities are available to partner and work with these corporations. Often, the supplier diversity and procurement processes need to be demystified for potential suppliers who may be unfamiliar with them, and employee resource groups are well-positioned to help small business owners navigate this effectively.

Each of these five pillars is an area of focus where employee resource groups can offer contributions and also receive the benefits of efforts focused on these key themes. They intersect and amplify in many areas, offering the potential for multilayered impact with a single activity (see figure 7). This is the value proposition of employee resource groups: impact in each of these areas at the same time.

Organizational leadership that can support employee resource groups and also infuse business goals around each of these areas will have a macro-level perspective on how ERGs can really benefit both employees and the organization. In the past, the connection and relationship between what employees offer in employee resource groups and how the business benefits has often not been entirely clear. As we reflect on these five pillars, I encourage you to be purposeful and intentional in clarifying both the goals of the business and how the employee resource group can benefit from interaction within the framing of these pillars.

The key to success and the opportunity for magnified impact is to have all of the engines around these pillars firing at the same time. However, in reality, there need to be priorities around which of these pillars are addressed and how. I advise employee resource groups

FIGURE 7. *INTERSECTING PILLARS OF ERGS.*

to first pick a few pillars and focus on addressing those well. Then, over time, add more objectives, goals, and activities related to other pillars, as is viable and comfortable for the group. At the same time, business leaders should bear in mind the big picture that ERGs can and should play an instrumental role in the enterprise, and that they need support and resources in order to maximize impact in each of these areas.

CONTEXT OF THE CURRENT TIMES

This framework for the pillars of your ERG is a conceptual model, but it does not exist in a vacuum. One must be mindful of the current times and what is on the minds of employees, organizational leadership, and the public. It would be tone-deaf to focus solely on business profitability at the expense of workplace and workforce engagement, particularly if employee morale is challenged by events in society at large. At the same time, employee resource groups cannot exclusively focus on social causes, as your ERGs are situated within companies that need to perform and deliver services. As a result, there needs to be a constant reevaluation and exploration of which of these pillars are a focus for each month and quarter for the employee resource groups. Determine priorities and then activate each pillar in alignment with them. Having everyone on board understand the nuanced interplay between what employee resource groups can *contribute* and how they can *benefit*—in the context of all these pillars—will promote productive conversations about where to allocate resources, time, and effort with the greatest potential impact.

That being said, employees are the carriers of culture and often shoulder the burdens of serving the community, colleagues, and the business all at the same time. There needs to be some recognition of the intensity of these roles, especially during times of challenge and change. Employee resource groups are often the go-to places for support, and the individuals who lead them are challenged by needing to manage their work responsibilities and the needs of their community at the same time.

The best way to ascertain if the ERG is going in the right direction is to make sure that there is a feedback loop of ongoing communication between ERGs, leadership, and human resources, and that goals and issues are transparently identified and shared. In addition to identifying goals and priorities and understanding how to operate your ERG, the next important topic is how to measure the effectiveness and impact of ERGs.

MEASURING IMPACT

Measuring the impact of employee resource groups and identifying and using appropriate metrics is one of the areas I receive the most questions about with regard to ERGs.

How do you gauge the impact of the ERG? It is critical to choose metrics that align with its goals and objectives—and to measure those intentions against actual outcomes.

What are some methods of measurement that are common among ERGs?

Commonly, organizations use indicators such as employee satisfaction surveys, DEI pulse surveys (brief, periodic surveys gauging inclusivity), diversity representation in departments, and other HR metrics to inform initiatives and chart progress. With ERGs, it is important to align with the overall organization's metrics but also to focus on assessments that connect directly to the membership and programming at hand. Common metrics include attendance at events, programmatic feedback forms, and surveys that gauge areas of interest and need. These measures are useful in better understanding ERG members and the populations that the ERG serves. There are other metrics that can stem from benchmarking a before-and-after state with employees' experience of inclusion and belonging.

An approach for demonstrating the impact of ERGs in a focused way would be to align the measurements with the pillars as listed above. How has the ERG delivered value in each of these key areas? Is there an opportunity to summarize and communicate what has already been achieved and what areas of growth are apparent? Having an ongoing way to share feedback and also measure progress will invite dialogue and exploration around the development of your ERG that is beneficial to all parties.

A number of common metrics can be used to assess the effectiveness and impact of employee resource groups.[3] Of course, these are dependent on your focus for the resource group and what vantage point you have as a stakeholder working with the ERG. Each stakeholder will pay attention to each metric differently. As a result, it is paramount to have an open conversation and be transparent about what is needed for the employee resource group to showcase its achievements and also receive support.

As an example of the varying degrees of importance assigned to metrics, a member of an ERG program committee would be very interested in how many attendees participated in an ERG event. The treasurer of that same ERG would be interested in seeing how much money was spent on event expenses and how many people were reached given those expenses, with a more analytical view of costs per head and budget for the fiscal year. An ERG chair may analyze both pieces of information in conjunction with some qualitative feedback that people felt more connected and supported during a particularly challenging time at the company and that there was an observable boost in morale. In order to show evidence for this qualitative impact, an ERG membership post-event survey could demonstrate how employee morale was enhanced through this event. This could be compared with a pulse survey sent prior to the event or a company-wide satisfaction survey that was administered by HR or DEI leadership. Given these pieces of information, one could make the case that employee resource groups contribute to overall organizational culture and employee engagement through their activities. As relevant pieces of information are gathered, tabulated, analyzed, and shared, the cost-benefit analysis may point to a net positive result from such ERG events.

A list of metrics and measures that are commonly used with employee resource groups is on the next page. These can be captured by the ERGs themselves, or by HR or DEI leaders. As you explore this list and select potential indicators, remember to align with the ERG pillars and also organizational objectives to make sure that you are focusing on key priorities.

SAMPLE METRICS AND MEASUREMENT
FOR EMPLOYEE RESOURCE GROUPS

Event attendance tracking

Costs and expenses over participants served

Number of partnering events with other ERGs and number of attendees

Employee satisfaction survey

Number of promotions of ERG members (compared with overall organizational baseline rate)

Number of participants in programs (for example, mentoring)

Employee retention by demographic group for ERG participants

Employee exits by demographic group for non-ERG participants

Dollars raised for community charitable giving

Number of attendees in skill development workshop

Qualitative feedback from workshop skill development experience

Number of committee members

Description of projects launched by employee resource groups

Input contributed to other departments (for example, Marketing, Research and Development)

Number of attendees at community career fair

Number of referrals of new small businesses interested in procurement process

Number of interested small businesses that convert into a vendor relationship

Feedback that has shaped HR policy

Number of participants in learning and development initiatives

Press and publicity for ERG initiatives

Attendance at industry conferences by ERG members

Speaking engagements at industry conferences by ERG members

Awards won by ERG or individual members

Photos and highlights from events and activities throughout the year

Quotes from executive sponsors and other senior leaders that express the impact of employee resource groups

Presence of CEO and other executives at ERG events

How do you choose which method of measurement is appropriate? Incorporate the flowchart shown in figure 8 in your decision-making about which metrics to use, and make sure to address each step in the process.

Visualize any of these metrics being summarized into an email to your executive sponsor or graphically represented in a quarterly or midyear report. All of these measures are ways to show the exciting accomplishments of employee resource groups and the impact that they can have on the entire organization.

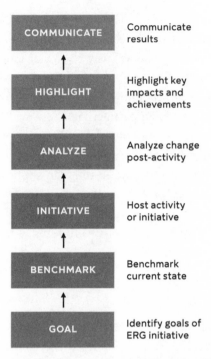

FIGURE 8. *IMPLEMENTING ERG MEASUREMENT AND METRICS.*

COMMUNICATION

Effectively communicating results through metrics and measurement is a key step in proving the value of an employee resource group's activities. ERGs often spend so much time on planning events that they run out of steam when it comes to conducting postevent documentation and communication of accomplishments. I advise all employee resource groups to have an ERG committee member in charge of postevent communications and ongoing evaluation and tracking of ERG activities.

Communications are vital for showcasing the activities, accomplishments, and impact of ERGs. It is absolutely essential to communicate with your executive sponsor and make sure that they share any key highlights with leaders of the company at their level.

Also, communication should be sent out company-wide for people who may not have attended the event or who may be interested in future activities. This is also a good way to garner more interest in membership for people who are observing how the group is going and exploring the idea of becoming involved in an employee resource group. Sharing highlights from past activities is a way to generate interest and excitement among potential ERG team members.

Collecting event and program highlights and summarizing key metrics produce valuable information that can support a midyear or year-end report by employee resource group leaders to key stakeholders. These reports can showcase the impact of ERGs and generate momentum for more resources, funding, and support for them in future years.

TECHNOLOGY

How do you keep all of these communications and evaluation processes active and effective, in a streamlined way? One option is to use centralized dashboards that track ERG member activity and can send out communications. These technological tools are powerful in enhancing the experience of employee resource groups through a single platform. Perhaps your organization has an intranet, a communications portal, or enterprise messaging tools already, and there can be a build-out to support your ERGs through various channels and areas in the platform. Or perhaps you have a team of engineers or communication specialists that can develop a platform in-house. This may be beneficial if your company has specific data security or functionality requirements and would prefer to have a purpose-built solution that meets those needs.

Another option is to purchase access to a third-party portal developed by vendors that specialize in HR, communications, event management, and ERG planning. As you consider what tool you would like to use, reflect on what your needs are and what you are trying to track, in relation to goals under each pillar. Of course, you have to consider the cost for these tools and determine if the organization has the budget for ongoing use of subscription-based offerings. They often have different levels of support and can provide various options, so it's wise to explore each of them and do a cost and services comparison to see which of them would be best suited for the needs of your ERGs.

As you assess the overall technology context of your organization and how employee resource groups are managed, most ERGs will require a combination of features, including shared document repositories, videoconferencing, and communication channels to meet, plan, and store information. Your team can develop a variety of spreadsheets and other tracking tools to record information and summarize data as needed.

All of these options around metrics and measurement tie back to the discussion at the start of the chapter around the purpose, people, processes, planning, and priorities of your ERGs. Make sure to consider your team's capabilities, and choose feasible metrics and measurements that will be sustainable over time. It is better to start small and grow rather than to take on more than is possible with the current team. Additionally, reviewing the pillars and ensuring that at least two or three of the most important ones are addressed is recommended. Quite often, an organization's DEI strategy will support involvement and engagement in all five pillars as a company-wide approach. Employee resource groups should feel empowered to offer support and guidance on any of the five pillars but also encourage greater organizational efforts around any pillar that needs more focus, attention, and support.

As a whole, incorporating the five pillars, selecting suitable metrics and measurement methods, and ensuring ongoing communication will create a winning strategy for ERGs. Allowing sufficient time for planning and prioritization will typically yield better results for your events and initiatives. However, if your ERG is already in flight with planning and implementing activities, it can be useful to pause and find some time to come together to affirm what the key areas of opportunity and focus are, in light of the applicable pillars, metrics, and communication channels for your employee resource group.

SIX

SOLIDARITY AND COMMUNITY BELONGING

PRESERVING SPACE AND SHOWING SOLIDARITY

As we have unfortunately seen repeatedly over time, current events have created the pressing need to provide a venue for gathering, healing, and offering empathy and support to individuals from underrepresented and marginalized groups. The pain of witnessing a traumatic news event that involves members of your own identity is inexpressible. There is a deep sense of loss, sadness, fear, anger, and resentment about the continued oppression and tragic events experienced by marginalized and underserved groups.

As an employee in the workplace, how can one safely process these emotions without being perceived as unprofessional or lacking in focus? How can one share honest thoughts about the disdain for systems and policies that has led to these tragic outcomes? How can employees share with their employers what they need without seeming inferior or less able to perform their job, in contrast with colleagues who may not be experiencing the same impacts from societal developments? Employee resource groups can play a role in answering these questions.

Employee resource groups serve as a place for employees to find solace in being able to process a common experience—such as an alarming news event—in the safety of a collective that is composed of others of the same identity grouping. Why is this important? As members face issues such as the harm and violence that result from racism, xenophobia, and systemic oppression, there is an urgent need to *preserve space* where they can gather, be in community, and offer support to one another. In spaces not specific to the demographic group, an unanticipated retraumatization can occur when members of other groups seek to explain the impact of these events on the communities who are experiencing them or observe members going through the pain at a distance, when they are not going through it themselves in the same way.

The horrific and tragic murder of George Floyd, ongoing violence against the Black community, and severe attacks against Asians sent companies into a tailspin as they tried to navigate how to support their employees. In my diversity, equity, and inclusion consulting work, I see firsthand how organizations have responded to these overwhelming events with a range of approaches and varying degrees of success. One large nonprofit organization whose CEO held community dialogue listening sessions for all employees was critiqued for not tailoring these sessions specifically to the Black community first. Leaders from a large corporation who put out a statement that they would donate to Asian community organizations were criticized because these actions were deemed performative. Other organizations held events led by their ERGs so that senior executives could hear stories directly from colleagues who were grieving or who felt unsafe to go outside due to the violent acts against their community.

Across the country, we saw the public push for engagement and accountability by organizations and an expectation that they would contribute to societal causes and transparently share their leadership diversity numbers through social media campaigns such as "Pull Up For Change." We lived in a frenzy of social media "Blackout" squares and hashtags, corporate statements of solidarity, and a rash of organizations' purchasing topical books, hiring diversity consultants, and promoting in-house personnel to new roles to address the urgent need to direct attention toward diversity, equity, and inclusion. Where did employee resource groups fit into all of this?

For many companies, employee resource groups served as a sounding board for how their diversity, equity, and inclusion efforts could more effectively address the populations affected. At the same time, ERGs rallied within their companies to make the case for why certain initiatives were imperative in order to address current needs and to take care of employees at their companies. The pivotal role that ERGs play in guiding organizations, being a resource for staff, and holding their organizations accountable for wider, transformative change is not often talked about. This dynamic of both serving and critiquing the company carries on and is amplified when societal matters pierce the workplace in their urgency and gravity.

ERGs occupy a unique position. On one hand, they can be an internal source of inspiration and can foster greater awareness and deeper impact. On the other hand, they can be perceived as a mechanism being used by companies to bypass current controversies and simply assuage their employees while they wait for the moment to pass. However, recent experience has proven that this moment is not a flash in the pan, and companies will not survive with a merely cursory approach to equity, inclusion, and change. What is needed and being called for are permanent, lasting, and sustainable ways to cultivate equity, belonging, and access for all, as well as accountability for actions toward these efforts.

ERGs are strong partners in helping to advance this mission. Their input has been invaluable and has—among other forms of impact—been conveyed through serving on company DEI committees, actively winning the support of employees for internal HR efforts, and frankly being resources for senior leadership and CEOs who are looking for guidance in how to proceed in the midst of instability and uncertainty. ERGs can be the source that leadership goes to first when crafting policies and statements. And if an ERG is sizable enough, it could allow minority employees to share critical feedback with less fear of individual retribution.

Given that ERGs have largely been an asset for companies and that leaders within ERGs have been a support to their members and employees who are wishing to be connected, what support is being provided for ERGs? What do ERGs need?

In a fantastic article for the *Harvard Business Review*, Aiko Bethea, a thought leader and consultant in the DEI field, talks about what Black employee resource groups need at this moment.[1] She outlines key areas that Black ERGs could use support in: equity and resources, transparency and trust, mental health support, and formal validation from leadership. She states, "Black ERGs are a clear pathway for organizations to offer support to Black employees. They are also a critical resource for information about what is and is not working for Black employees. Valuing, supporting, and sustaining a Black ERG is a win-win for the company and those they aim to support."

There is much research that shows the necessity of organizations to establish psychological safety in the workplace to help it thrive. This is needed now more than ever as continued challenges with wellness, mental health, work-life balance, and polarization around key issues have led to a lack of safety in the workplace on many fronts. Organizations that foster genuine inclusion—and allow for existing organizational norms to be safely critiqued without risk of retribution—will find that they thrive. Employees will feel more likely to be involved, to be engaged, and to contribute to their fullest potential. Employee resource groups promote psychological safety in the safe spaces they create and offer a united front to challenge organizational norms that may be unsupportive of members of certain groups.

One aspect of what ERGs can provide for psychological safety is the ability to collectively gather and heal. This can be done by offering supportive EAP (employee assistance program) resources for therapy and clinical resources. Some companies have hosted "wellness rooms" where individuals gather and speak about their emotions and process how they are feeling.

One program I have instituted in organizations is healing sessions led by healer-facilitators who cultivate spaces in the form of intimate gatherings—in person or virtual—where there can be an expression of emotion and a somatic release of any energetic imprint that was accumulated from the trauma and mental or emotional anguish felt by marginalized communities. Organizations that are our clients participate in these unique sessions to foster processing and recovery within their designated community groupings. The results of these gatherings are phenomenal. There is so much impact in coming together to intentionally support and heal one another. This can help release any anxiety about working with others or being able to deal with the overwhelming experiences of recent times.

One large company had a challenging relationship with its employees of color who asked for transparency around DEI initiatives and what would be done by the company to advocate for decisions and actions that supported marginalized communities' members. The psychological impacts on employees of color from race relations flashpoints in society—coupled with a lack of trust felt by these employees in their workplace—created a sense of urgency for action. As a part of the strategic planning process, we established ongoing training and coaching support for senior leaders and all staff, and also incorporated healing sessions for BIPOC-identified and White-identified members of the company. These healing sessions helped center the needs of the individuals in their own identities and methods of processing and helped release the energetic layers of the heaviness of the moment. After these sessions, individuals and the group collectively were able to come together to establish trust and find a way forward. They also had strengthened leadership within their ERGs to direct this renewed collective purpose toward cultivating equity in their company and the industry overall.

The University of Colorado Denver invited me to plan and host a series of healing sessions for their multiracial and biracial students' association, which was an affinity group on campus to support individuals of multiple races and ethnicities. This series allowed students, faculty, and staff to gather and be a part of sessions geared toward their personal experiences based on racialization and polarization, as well as the experience of being of mixed race in a world where they may be misperceived or misunderstood by others. The first two sessions focused on healing around racial experiences and the dynamics of being multiracial in a racially charged and polarized environment, and participants remarked how this space was supportive and healing of what they had been going through.

However, immediately before our third session, we received updates about a terrible mass shooting in the state. The attendees at our third session were grateful to have the space to process the current struggles they were facing around racial experiences, the fear of going outside, and also the re-traumatization of recalling previous instances of mass shootings and hesitancy to go to the movie theater because of previous tragedies. Having supportive spaces in which affinity groups can gather helps support the participants in an ongoing way and can be instrumental in addressing difficult events as they unfold and are experienced in real time by those at your organization.

In both of these examples, establishing trust and providing spaces for collective gathering and healing was pivotal to the group's ability to address current issues and move forward with solutions and resources that were trauma informed and mindful of the needs of the participants involved. Ideally, these events and programs are planned in an ongoing way, so that there is a decreased stigma around mental health needs, and wellness programs are not viewed as solely a reactive tool deployed in response to unfortunate tragic events but rather as a proactive part of our everyday approach to self-care, work, and life.

If preserving space for individuals of a particular demographic group is needed, how do individuals who are not members of that group participate and support? All employee resource groups should be open to members of all demographic groups. This should be an established, company-wide policy and clearly stated in ERG membership guidelines. That said, how do allies actively participate without dominating the conversation or taking up space?

This is a frequently asked question in my work with employee resource groups. The way to address this is for ERGs to create some events that are open to all and others that are for the demographic group only. This gives an opportunity for the wider organization to take part in events that can support the particular demographic. It also allows for a community to have its own space yet also be supported by members outside of that demographic. The same can apply to organizational leaders and DEI and HR representatives who wish to participate but also leave space for the ERG members to have dialogue and discussion.

One stellar example of how senior leaders can be effective allies comes from Seth Smiley-Humphries, Chief Diversity Officer at GE Hitachi and former Director of Inclusion and Diversity at ONE Gas and Global Director of Diversity and Inclusion at Lenovo, who identifies as White and has a male partner and a biracial child. At a conference I was hosting, Seth shared with the audience how he would attend events for the Black employee resource group at Lenovo: he would greet the group, give welcoming remarks, and then leave the event so that Black ERG members could meet among themselves. Another ERG for BIPOC members I am currently advising has a White female executive sponsor who is quite active and involved. She often attends the first 15 minutes of the monthly meetings to share any updates, answer questions, and offer support, and then departs the meeting. She is involved in a regular cadence of meeting with the BIPOC employee resource group leaders, and this is a way that senior leaders can show allyship even though they are of an identity different than the focus of the group itself.

As for employees who are not of the identity group of a particular ERG, I have witnessed many individuals of various demographic groups joining employee resource groups of their interest. Sometimes this can be advantageous to the ERG, as they may need support in officer roles. A colleague of mine who is Latino and White and works at a large medical technology company is the father of an adopted son who is Black, and even outside of that he is generally eager to support the Black community. He is very involved in advocacy for the Black community and participates regularly in the company ERG events in a sensitive and informed way.

Employee resource groups cannot and should not exist without participation and support from their allies! The key is how to effectively engage allies to play a role that does not take away from the primary purpose of supporting the demographic at hand.

We have talked about preserving space for demographic groups of ERGs and how to engage allies. What about how employee groups can work together? Cross-collaboration among ERGs should be a top priority for ERGs themselves as well as for company leaders. There are tremendous benefits to cross-collaboration among ERGs. The demonstration of solidarity and support across groups is critical, now and always. As ERGs confront challenges in society, there is a need to come together and show support for one another during times when community groups are in struggle.

Also, it is important to show solidarity and allyship across groups to model community building and unity across key issues. In the case of the movement for Black lives and the increased attention on attacks against Asians, there was the opportunity for solidarity building among these communities that were stricken with violence against their communities and ongoing loss. Events promoting solidarity across groups can also help address deeper issues of anti-Black racism and anti-Asian racism and other intense matters that can exist in all communities. This collaborative approach helps deepen and strengthen connections among community groups and also demonstrates how ERGs can come together to fight against weighty issues of systemic racism and oppression and to partner in creating more belonging and support within organizations.

I witnessed an example of cross-collaboration in the concept of a "handoff" event. ERG leaders at a tech company wrapping up Asian Americans and Pacific Islanders (AAPI) Heritage month in May and moving into Pride Month in June created a "handshake" event cohosted by the AAPI ERG and the LGBTQIA+ ERG to foster the movement from one heritage month to another. This was such a creative way to overtly showcase the collaboration and connectedness across ERGs.

Another benefit to cross-collaboration is the sharing of resources. Given budgetary challenges, pooling funds and also jointly leveraging a multitude of resources, such as sharing venue costs and cohosting an event to drive greater attendance, are ways that cross-collaboration can benefit all groups involved. I have spoken with many senior leaders at organizations who favor events and programs that involve more than one ERG, for the aforementioned reasons.

I can share my own experience being a part of employee resource groups and cross-collaboration: I am often asked to do an author talk on my book *Raising Multiracial Children: Tools for Nurturing Identity in a Racialized World* and lead a session for ERGs called "How to Talk to Kids About Race." I have been enthused to see employee resource groups from various racial demographics come together and cohost this event, along with their parenting-focused ERG. I have always felt proud to be a part of these events because they involve ERGs from many different backgrounds coming together to talk about important issues, something we can all galvanize support around. These events are often well attended, and I hear feedback afterward about how they help strengthen relationships among ERGs in this active showing of solidarity among the different groups.

In this chapter, we discussed why it is important to preserve space for demographic groups within ERGs, how allies can take part in ERGs, and how to show solidarity and cross-collaboration among groups. I end here with some related questions for you to consider as you plan ERG events and programs throughout the year.

As you reflect on these questions, I encourage you to make an effort to encourage a variety of different experiences for your members and to work with other ERGs. Being intentional in this way models the solidarity and collaboration that are needed across organizations to foster belonging and connection among all.

QUESTIONS FOR REFLECTION: PRESERVING SPACE AND SUPPORTING SOLIDARITY

How does your organization address current events and traumatic news? What is your protocol for responding?

How are ERGs sensitively utilized as a resource to advise on these issues? How can they be involved without being expected to take on additional labor?

What spaces for healing and collective gathering are in place at your organization? What can be created to support the emotional and mental health of your employees, while consciously acknowledging their identities as part of that planning and preparation?

How are allies of groups positioned to sensitively engage and support other demographic groups?

What cross-collaboration and solidarity-building initiatives are underway at your organization? How can there be more connection across affinity groups, so that each group is supported and resources and ideas can be pooled and shared?

SEVEN

BEST PRACTICES AND COMMON PITFALLS

OVERCOMING CHALLENGES AND FINDING YOUR WAY

What are some obstacles you have faced in your role with your employee resource group? How have you overcome those challenges? What does and doesn't work for your group? In this chapter, we will explore some common areas of concern when running employee resource groups and best practices for how to operate your ERG more effectively.

There can be some need for clarity as to what an ERG's role is with respect to business lines in the company. Consider the previous example of a wireless communications company that was eager to get its latest products into the hands of a certain demographic group and decided to have its ERG host an in-person event with give-aways of the product, as well as a social mixer for the ERG to meet external community members. This was an innovative idea to build relationships among community stakeholders as well as the public, with a particular targeted demographic. The experience from the public was positive, and the ERG leaders were eager to share some of the critical feedback about how to improve the marketing campaign to better engage members of this demographic. The marketing team at this wireless communications company felt that some of the requests and input went beyond the ERG members' role and were less interested in working together in the future. This impacted the ERG leaders' and marketing leaders' relationship. What would you have done to prevent such a potential misunderstanding?

This case shows how there weren't clear goals and expectations moving into this event regarding how the ERG and the marketing team should work together. Perhaps that clarity could have come from holding more joint meetings beforehand or from communication between the ERG's executive sponsor and the business line leader in charge of marketing that would be impacted by this feedback. The issue at hand is when the ERGs, in their eager attempt to support the company, move into the roles of others who work there. This can cause friction and unintended misunderstandings.

As a best practice, it is important that the roles and positions of employee resource group leaders and their programs support the company and that community outreach is welcomed as an added benefit, but that ERGs don't intrude into the role and function of a particular department in the organization.

The reverse can also happen, where ERGs are asked to go above and beyond their role as volunteer employee leaders. Due to the identities and lived experience of ERG leaders, they are sometimes tapped to make decisions about company-wide DEI strategy and shape decisions and actions on behalf of the entire organization. Although it is important to receive feedback from ERG leaders and their groups, this could be an overburdening of the ERG leaders and an addition of labor that ERG leaders should not be expected to carry.

An example of this is when a financial institution that wanted to roll out a learning and development initiative on diversity, equity, and inclusion was constantly tapping its ERG leaders to spread the word about the optional informational sessions. Although it was a way to engage members of the organization who might not normally have been as involved or heard about these events, it placed undue burden on the ERG members to perform the outreach on behalf of this campaign. A better way to launch these DEI efforts would have been to go through each department's management and encourage participation via supervisors and their direct reports. This example shows a larger challenge with DEI efforts not having enough support or enough value for their launch to gain traction and be taken seriously.

Another example is a human rights advocacy nonprofit organization that was resistant to doing a company-wide survey on DEI. The DEI committee was on board, as was HR, but some senior executive team members were not. The employees from underrepresented groups had to rally together to give feedback to the DEI committee to showcase the benefits of the survey—namely giving voice to topics not previously discussed—and overcome the fear and resistance of the senior leadership. This example shows the effectiveness of ERG members coming together but also how it can be an added burden and may reveal a larger issue around the approach to DEI at the company overall.

A concern for ERGs to guard against is the unintended preferential treatment toward those who are salaried workers or are based at the headquarters or main office who can participate in ERG work, whereas others cannot. Organizations may have many employees spread out across the country and around the world, and ERG programming must be mindful of time zones, constraints of shift work, and other aspects of logistical planning that can impact participation and attendance. The inclusion of all employees should be top of mind for ERG leaders. However, there may be constraints on how to encourage participation.

For example, there may be a need for a new company-wide policy that pays for time during which hourly workers show up for ERG meetings and events beyond their regular shifts. Some companies may refrain from formalizing efforts to cultivate that participation for ERGs and may dismiss this as too much work or something that requires legal attention and therefore may take a long time to approve. It is important to avoid head office bias—favoring the main office or headquarters—and minimize these constraints, so that there is wider outreach and the ability for individuals to participate who may otherwise not be able to. This is how we aim to detect and eradicate bias in organizational policies and decisions and how leaders can endeavor to make the workplace more equitable and inclusive.

A GLOBAL WORKFORCE

A best practice to engage a workforce with employees who may have different shifts or be in a variety of geographic locations is to rotate meeting times and dates, so that the start time of one meeting can be early for some and late for others, and then have the next meeting start at a decent time for some but early or late for others, and so on.

Other aspects of cross-cultural interaction are also important to keep in mind as you enter new relationships and perhaps work together across global groups. The need for cultural intelligence and intercultural understanding cannot be underscored enough! An American company that recently acquired a company based in Europe was met with differences in communication styles and orientation toward understanding information. There was a marked difference in how individuals from each country paid attention to getting to know one another, as well as in spending time on the philosophy and intellectual debate around an idea versus getting right down to action and decision-making. This intercultural dimension of task versus relationship is a common difference that can plague new groups from different countries working together; it can impact how work is effectively conducted and can lead to misunderstanding. Similarly, employee resource group members can face problems in coordinating with their ERG counterparts in other countries if these norms of communication are not brought to awareness and understood.

Additionally, the logistical structure of how ERGs report in to headquarters can cause some groups that are not physically close to headquarters to be unintentionally left out of enterprise-wide initiatives. This can impact participation in major organizational events, who is chosen as an ERG leader, and even how an ERG can influence senior leaders or executives to move a large program or idea along.

One manufacturing company I was advising had a strong women's network that was based out of their headquarters in Michigan, which enabled proximity to their HR leader, who was personally very involved in the group. Due to this, they received significant extra support with their ERG initiatives, and the ERG flourished and grew. The ERGs from other demographic groups that had leaders based in Atlanta and the new locations of Hong Kong and the UK hadn't established that relationship with headquarters in the same way and weren't receiving the same support from the HR leader and the company overall. As mergers and acquisitions happen, and companies are acquired, organizations have to go through constant transition and onboarding, and they need to be mindful of how to include members and participants from various regions, demographic groups, and cultures.

Related to this, there are new employees joining the company at any time. I once observed how a new employee—after attending an ERG meeting for the first time—felt that it wasn't right for her, because the ERG leaders were so focused on discussing ongoing internal company matters. It is sometimes difficult to remember to welcome new members at every meeting and find a way to incorporate those who are new into the group, but it must be done. There should be a recommended script in opening the meeting, welcoming new members, sharing where individuals can go for questions and support, and welcoming any input and feedback at the end. This will ensure that new members do not feel left out and have a sense of direction as to the purpose of the ERG, how they can get involved, and how the overall organization interacts with the ERG. The meeting I witnessed was an intense discussion around how BIPOC employees were being treated at the company that involved a critique of the industry, a dialogue that had been going on for some time. Looking back, I think the ERG leaders could have seen how, without the appropriate framing, this might be an intense topic for someone who was new to the company and came to this ERG meeting on the first week of her job!

ENSURING ACCESS AND SUCCESSION PLANNING: THE INEQUITY OF CUPCAKES

The impact of not being in physical proximity to the head office is far-reaching—even as a result of the most unexpected circumstances.

One organizational client I partner with has a collaboration with a bakery that donates baked goods to volunteer leaders at their nonprofit agency. In DEI focus groups that we conducted, we heard from various employees about how they didn't get to receive the cupcakes because they were not on-site at the main campus. Even though this gesture of sharing the bakery items was a positive one, it actually led to inequity, with some people feeling left out. As ERGs and company senior leaders navigate working together—especially with employees at other locations—there must be mindfulness about how to engage individuals who are working remotely or are at various locations.

Another pitfall of ERGs is succession planning in how ERG leader transitions are prepared for and handled. Depending on how the ERG is set up and how it is managed by the company, there may not be clear succession planning to appoint and onboard a new ERG team member. This can cause some difficulty with ERG leaders who are not trained or properly equipped to take on the new role. An ERG leader who has been in the role for many years can also present a challenge. This can cause a strain on the ERG because other members may not feel that they are qualified or have enough tenure to step up and take on a role, in contrast with someone who has been there for a very long time. The solution is to have clear term limits, to ensure that there is a pipeline for leadership that is nurtured, and that future leaders are supported and guided before they take on formal positions. There is also the potential risk of institutional knowledge not being passed on when ERG leadership changes. This can cause difficulty if an ERG leader leaves and takes the deep knowledge of the group and the organization with them, without any transition plan or sharing of best practices or knowledge of key relationships with other stakeholders that can help the resource group team work together effectively.

In this chapter, we talked about common challenges and considerations in leading an ERG. This includes defining what is beyond the role of the ERG leader and can intrude into the business functions of the company, as well as engaging staff members at different levels in the organization (including hourly and shift workers), along with international workers or those who are in different geographic locations. We also discussed how a lack of succession planning can interrupt the transfer of institutional knowledge and can also leave an ERG without a pipeline of talent to fill its internal leadership roles.

···

QUESTIONS FOR REFLECTION: ERG PRACTICES

• What aspects of your ERG intersect or overlap with business functions (such as learning and development, marketing, organizational strategy) in a way that can cause tension, conflict, or misunderstanding? How can you relieve the burden of responsibility from the ERG leaders? How can you ensure that ERG efforts don't compromise the relationships and functioning of the business if they penetrate into some organizational functions?

• How does your company engage with hourly and shift workers? Are there policies and guidelines in place for how hourly and shift workers can participate in ERG events and activities (such as flex time or overtime for taking part)?

- How does your company cultivate inclusion and belonging for a global workforce? What cross-cultural considerations need awareness and dialogue as you enter relationships across borders?

- What succession-planning initiatives are in place for your ERG leaders to ensure that institutional knowledge is passed on? How are potential new leaders being nurtured and onboarded throughout the ERG's life span?

EIGHT

ERGS AS OPPORTUNITIES

CULTIVATING CREATIVITY AND GROWTH

Employee resource groups have been at the forefront of organizational innovation since their inception. They have advanced the dialogue around equity and inclusion, uplifted issues that needed to be heard, and continue to delicately navigate organizational dynamics to allow for careful consideration of the needs of their members. ERGs are living organisms within organizations that serve as the conduit for conversation and the glue between groups and individuals that normally don't have an opportunity to interact.

THE ERG AS CAREER BOOSTER

One of the top reasons why ERGs hold potential for organizational impact is grounded in how they nurture leaders by offering a venue for developing leadership experience, how they can assist with advancing careers, and how they are containers from which innovation can grow and thrive.

Let's start with career advancement.

There could be employees at your company who don't normally get exposed to parts of the business and may be interested in building a new skill or learning about a role they don't currently have exposure to. An ERG fosters cross-pollination of ideas and people, allowing for informal interaction, networking, and shadowing through the relationships that form and grow within the group. I was coaching a senior woman of color at a well-known restaurant company who wanted to advance her career and was considering learning a new function in the business. At the time, she was in charge of visiting the franchise store owners and was on the ground with vendors and suppliers, but she wanted a more corporate role in human resources and diversity and inclusion. She was able to leverage her contacts within her ERG to get in touch with a senior company leader in HR and set up an informational interview to learn more about opportunities and also express her interest in this new arena. That meeting went well, and she then tapped her company's professional development funding to gain new certifications that would help her with a potential new role. She is working her way toward a career change and is well recognized as a leader within her ERG, with visibility from other senior leaders who are familiar with her work and efforts. The value of connection within the ERG and also visibility with senior leaders who see her commitment, interest, and quality of work are very apparent. This is the power and impact that ERGs can have in navigating organizations and accessing resources that can boost your career.

Second, ERGs are great places to practice leadership and develop skills like project management and public speaking. I have witnessed time and again how employees who are not confident in their abilities are able to practice and expand their leadership skills in so many new ways, all due to their participation in their ERG. Many members and leaders of ERGs have shared with me how they have learned to take risks in their ERG roles—by exploring new dimensions of leadership that they hadn't before—and that they have learned so much and benefited from that experience.

At the same time, senior leaders in the company and direct managers and supervisors of employees participating in ERGs can also see and chart that growth within them. The leaders may even nominate their employees to a leadership or committee role in the

ERG to foster talent development. It is a win-win for employees to take part in ERGs and advance their own leadership skills through organizing ERG activities, while contributing to company initiatives that in turn benefit overall belonging and engagement of employees in the workplace. It is an extremely effective cycle of learning, contributing, growth, and development.

To take this idea of ERGs as career boosters one step further, I can share with you what senior executive leaders at numerous organizations have told me during candid conversations: they look to employee resource groups as places to find talent and fill roles. ERGs are extremely effective promotional pathways for individuals who contribute and are engaged and involved. ERGs serve as a shortcut for identifying candidates who would best suit a new role or lead a new team. The process of sourcing talent from ERGs allows the senior leader to receive feedback from various stakeholders—from colleagues, peers, other leaders, and even the executive sponsor—about a particular person's performance, and that can go miles in terms of consideration for a promotion or advancement within the company in a new role.

THE ERG AS A SANDBOX FOR INNOVATION: CREATIVITY AT PLAY

ERGs are also a sandbox for innovation! A lot of play and creativity can happen in an ERG that may not otherwise be feasible across departments and within vertical units as they are conventionally set up in companies. As an analogy, Pixar created large common spaces to promote creative integration and exchange of ideas across departments. I see ERGs as an organic vehicle for that to happen in an intentional way.

An example of this comes from DEI initiatives at The Clorox Company, led by Erby L. Foster, Chief Diversity and Inclusion Officer at the company. Foster actively worked with Clorox's ERGs around employee engagement as well as product innovation. In the past, the company held friendly competitions within their ERGs around who could develop new products to serve the public, from the perspective of different communities that the ERGs represented. A few notable products came from those competitions. One was the stackable lids for plastic storage containers that took the market by storm and are still extremely popular today. Another was the colored filter jug for the Brita brand that the company markets, which was very popular with East Asian and South Asian consumers, as it was launched in conjunction with the major occasions of Lunar New Year and Diwali, and the colors red and orange are auspicious for those communities.

Foster describes the impact of ERGs on the business, saying, "ERGs have helped Clorox reach diverse consumers through their cultural insights. We've also leveraged this ERG business mindset to build stronger relationships with our customers. Working with a diverse group of people, then, is a great way to increase creativity. Even though this may seem like an obvious truth, it is remarkable how seldom we apply it. Creating a culture of inclusion is most definitely a competitive business advantage."[1] Erby Foster is describing the lasting contributions ERGs can make on the business, on the larger public, and also in product innovation. Creativity comes from fostering a close connection among individuals from a similar background and can help introduce new market insights as well as serve a customer need. Employees, customers, leaders, and the public all benefit from the collaboration that ERGs offer.

A further example comes from Hallmark, where then–Director of Diversity and Inclusion, Michael Gonzales, supported the engaging of the LGBTQIA+ employee resource group to come up with a line of inclusive greeting cards that pictured same-sex couples and non-binary identity, which was launched in conjunction with merchandising at the Walgreens store located in the Castro District in San Francisco.[2] This was so well received by the community in that local area that it brought tears to people's eyes in deep recognition of being seen, understood, valued, and represented in these products.

Reflecting on this moment and his entire career supporting DEI within organizations, Gonzales shares this wisdom: "The drive for diversity, equity, and inclusion is not an event. There is no finish line. It is an ongoing and ever-changing journey fueled by passion."[3] This absolutely illustrates the spirit behind employee resource groups. The passion of members, the leaders who support them, and the communities they serve is palpable at every event hosted by ERGs. In this example, we can also see how challenges can turn into opportunities. Gonzales goes on to say, "Diversity, Equity, and Inclusion is a journey, and with any journey you find strength to forge ahead. You look for influences or experiences that validate your conviction and affirm you're on the right path. Our responsibility is to mentor and create new experiences for those coming after us." This truly captures the sentiment behind company leaders and executive sponsors who take on the responsibility to support employee resource groups, as well as ERG leaders themselves. Without this support and dedication, ERGs would not be able to operate as effectively as they do."

These examples show how ERGs generated valuable ideas and immediately benefited the business through careful consideration, dialogue, and the ability to be creative and imagine new possibilities. The positive effects of ERGs are far-reaching across both internal and external stakeholders, ranging from enhanced engagement, inclusion, and belonging among employees to positive brand perception and sentiment on the part of current and potential future customers.

The above stories illustrate the innovation that can arise from ERGs and the impact that can be created, but there are so many more examples. How has your ERG provided fertile ground for innovation and creativity to thrive? The opportunities are endless.

·····

The drive for diversity, equity, and inclusion is not an event. There is no finish line. It is an ongoing and ever-changing journey fueled by passion.
—Michael Gonzales, DEI Director, Hallmark

·····

COMPANY CULTURE INTEGRATION DURING MERGERS

A large public relations company I was working with on the East Coast acquired a smaller tech company based in Texas. There was energy and excitement around the coming together of these teams, with strong leadership among all the ERG members, the DEI lead, and business line leaders at each company. As I was advising the ERG leaders, it became apparent that similar diversity initiatives were being pursued at both the larger company and the acquired start-up. The question was, how to align and combine the existing ERGs?

This could be approached as a tactical question, and as we looked at it this way to start, the first thing I advised the two companies to do was adopt a common calendar so that the ongoing initiatives by each ERG (Pride, Multigenerational, Women, and so on) could be supported at each location and so that individuals at various locations could participate in all events they were eager to join. Second, we looked at how the norms and organizational culture of each of the companies would come together. Some initiatives around yoga and meditation happened at one company that were not present in the other company, and there was a movement toward wellness that was adopted by all, with intentional efforts. There were also contrasts around gathering socially tied to company culture that needed to be worked out. We observed how the immediate collaboration and connection among the ERGs helped with the integration of company culture during this time of significant corporate change.

If your company is going through a merger or acquisition, what steps is it taking to ensure that the integration of culture is seamless,

....

ERGs can be the glue that binds together a company culture made up of segments that were distinct and separate to start.

....

and how are ERGs involved with that transition? There are many opportunities to engage employees across companies that are coming together via a merger or acquisition, through the vehicle of employee resource groups and joint activities and initiatives. Although it will take some adjustment to combine the cultures and methods of convening that could be different across companies, ERGs can be the glue that binds together a company culture made up of segments that were distinct and separate to start.

GREATER SOCIAL IMPACT AND ALIGNMENT WITH MOVEMENTS

Companies have a tremendous ability to influence society through their public policies and stances toward societal issues. ERGs can influence and help guide companies in these matters. We have witnessed how far-reaching social movements have forced companies to take a stand, to make commitments to social and racial justice and to equity and inclusion within their operations, and also to serve as models to society overall.

ERG leaders and members have been key advisors to organizations as they ascertain where to invest funds for charitable causes, how to engage with the public in an authentic and effective way, and how best to serve fellow employees as they move through the turmoil of major life-changing events in society.

The approach to contributing to and aligning with social movements needs to be carefully considered and properly executed. A public relations–heavy response—for example, with charitable donations and public statements—may feel right in the short term but could appear to be offering empty promises for visibility and performance in the long term. I recall advising a CEO who was motivated and inspired to write a statement in support of the ongoing racial justice movement and the movement for Black lives. His employees were inspired by it—and at the same time they questioned him and his team about what was next. It is all too common to feel motivated to respond but not to have all the details figured out.

A purposeful strategy around DEI, connecting with social causes and also incorporating valuable ERG input, is the recommended approach.

Social impact can also be driven by organizations that ERG leaders and members are a part of. One such example comes from Jimmy Hua, Cofounder and Leader of the Asian Leaders Alliance (ALA), which is a collective of members of ERGs from the Asian and Pacific Islander community across various companies.[4] Reflecting on the time of the heightened violent attacks against Asians, Hua shares, "ERG members within ALA noticed that many companies struggled with what to do after the Atlanta shooting. And many of the API ERG leaders also struggled with what to advise their employer to do. A half dozen leads got together and created a slide show and template on what to advise their executive leadership on what to do based on the collective experiences of those making the resources. That empowered dozens of ERG leaders to enable their executive leadership to take action publicly and help their employees internally. This also influenced millions of dollars to be donated to API organizations that needed the help."

I personally was a part of the emergency meetings that were formed in response to the rising attacks against Asians, and I facilitated a delicate space-holding gathering to support Asian and Pacific Islander ERG leaders who were troubled and traumatized by the violent events and yet had to lead initiatives at their companies. I witnessed how this ERG community banded together to share resources and come up with a response that they could take back to their company leaders to give their organizations direction. ALA also saw an increase in membership at the time, with a record number of Asian-based ERGs forming at organizations that year.

Hua states that "ERGs are currently evolving to be strategic in what they do instead of just doing events" and "ERGs cannot just wait for opportunities. Instead they need to prepare for those opportunities and have a game plan." In this case, the opportunities for ERGs stemmed from tragedy and sorrow, but the ALA collective was able to support ERG leaders and members to strategically address the issue and lead toward sustainable initiatives at their company over time. As we can see, there can be an external social cause that is the catalyst for ERG growth.

ERGS AND PUBLIC POLICY

In multiple visits to the White House as a community representative and stakeholder regarding minority entrepreneurship and employee resource groups over the past decade, I was part of an effort to demonstrate how concerted action from small business advocacy organizations, community groups, ERGs, corporations, and government can contribute to greater inclusion, access, and equity for all. These joint summits illuminated key issues and fostered understanding across stakeholder groups, allowing for deep dialogue around concerns for the lack of minority representation in leadership at the highest levels of public office and industry. Attention was paid to pressing challenges comprehensively, engaging stakeholders of all levels, and dissecting issues so that they could be addressed in purposeful and actionable ways. ERG leaders and members were at the forefront of those conversations.

One particular leader who makes an admirable impact in this space is Mohammed Farshori, Director of Citizenship and Sustainability at AT&T. He is responsible for managing, building, and expanding global community and employee engagement efforts across Europe, the Middle East, and Africa (EMEA), as well as the Asia-Pacific (APAC) region. Farshori is also the past National President of the AT&T employee resource group called OASIS (Organization of Asian Indians at AT&T) and Cofounder and COO of AT&T's newest ERG, Faith@Work. I have seen Farshori attend and present at White House ERG summits on a number of occasions and have visited the AT&T headquarters in Dallas, Texas. What I have learned from Farshori is how companies such as AT&T are active supporters of employees and the identities they hold through ERGs, and how a sound corporate structure and involvement with public affairs and community initiatives readily encourage this. AT&T has an impressive track record of engaging its people with public issues such as disaster response preparedness, together creating solutions that benefit the community. ERGs give leaders such as Mohammed Farshori the opportunity to steward important initiatives that bring about change and betterment both within the organization and around the world.

Involvement in ERGs gives leaders across industries a platform to raise concerns and to continue the conversation and development across key stakeholders in corporate, government, nonprofit, and entrepreneur networks. This connection to public policy is critical, and ERG leaders can be influencers to shape policy to support specific goals through their relationships and presence in the public sphere.

NEW FRONTIERS

There are causes that we haven't fully addressed and are still in the process of further exploration, brainstorming, and decision-making. What can be surfaced from employees, the public, and employee resource groups? ERGs can be an avenue for that continued dialogue and discovery.

One such development is related to the reproductive health of employees. Zomato, a food-delivery start-up in India, implemented a new policy that introduced an allowance for paid time off for menstruating employees. This was an effort to be more inclusive to women and to transgender and non-binary individuals and give them the opportunity to take time off without having to use vacation or sick days. I was quoted in *Marie Claire* addressing this issue, emphasizing how ERGs globally could take this up within their respective organizations and offer support and insights.[5] Menstrual health days are recognized in Japan and South Korea, but there is no such widespread policy for menstrual leave at organizations in many other countries.

Reproductive health could be addressed more comprehensively, including offering time off for miscarriage and hormone-replacement therapy. So much about reproductive and menstrual health is stigmatized, and employees have to face the emotional and physical impacts of these issues, in addition to having to navigate them in the work-place, in the absence of systems and policies that can support them. It is also in the interest of companies to offer these benefits to employees to mitigate the financial loss of lowered productivity or turnover as a result of a lack of inclusion and equitable benefits for individuals with these needs. This is a tremendous opportunity for companies and ERGs to address in partnership toward effective policies and solutions.

Although some of these topics may seem as if they are pushing boundaries, don't forget that some rights, like maternity leave and parental leave for partners, were adopted only in recent decades, in no small part due to the advocacy of groups who were committed to these causes and fought hard against the norms of the time to create opportunity, equity, and benefits for those who needed them. At the same time, we are in this current moment when many challenges need to be addressed. ERGs are a method of galvanizing support around an issue that could benefit from the attention, focus, and guidance of concerned members. Company leaders need not fear the uncharted territory and should instead welcome the conversation. The more pro-active that organizations can be regarding these topics, the more they will be known as employers of choice in the battle for talent, exper-tise, and valuable perspectives that come from a diverse workforce.

As we have covered in this chapter, employee resource groups have the potential to unlock the door of opportunity in many ways. ERGs can be career boosters for employees, offering possibilities for con-necting with other leaders, practicing new skills, and gaining exposure to new parts of the business, as well as acting as a promotional path-way for ERG leaders. ERGs can be a sandbox where creativity and innovation thrive. New product offerings and innovative approaches to the business can be cultivated through formal and informal devel-opment of ideas. ERGs offer the opportunity for greater social impact by connecting to causes, addressing government policy in partnership with other societal stakeholders, and also addressing pioneering topics around equity and access within companies.

The profound impact of employee resource groups goes beyond perceiving them simply as a gathering of employees from the same identity group. Organizations with successful DEI and ERG initiatives understand this. As Erby Foster describes: "Diversity isn't as simple as grouping together different races, genders, or cultural backgrounds. It's about building an inclusive team with assorted thoughts and beliefs, to create a more comprehensive solution to global business issues. Even though this seems like an obvious truth, it's remarkable how seldom we apply it."[6] Employee resource groups create the environment for powerful, impactful ideas to form, and for robust solutions to arise, to meet any challenges.

The possibilities for ERGs to create impact in all these ways are limitless. As you consider the possibilities for ERGs at your own organization, take a moment to reflect individually and with your team as to which goals and opportunities are apparent and how ERGs can support initiatives to that end.

QUESTIONS FOR REFLECTION: OPPORTUNITIES FOR CREATIVITY AND GROWTH

- How can ERGs be career boosters for people at your company or for you individually?

- How can ERGs serve as promotional pathways for members of your group?

- How can ERGs be a sandbox for innovation, creativity, and productive development? And for developing and practicing leadership skills?

- How can ERGs support the transition of culture and integration of companies during mergers and acquisitions?

- How can your ERG impact society through alignment with social movements, influencing local and national government policy, and helping take pioneering stances on issues?

NINE

SHAPING THE FUTURE NOW

THE POWER AND POTENTIAL OF ERGS

We began this book thinking about how transformational change can occur through the engagement of key stakeholders, including organizational leaders, employees, and the public. As we think about the future of employee resource groups, what are the issues that are left to explore further? And how do we continue to create authentic change in a sustainable and long-term way? Employee resource groups can be both the source and the method for initiating transformational change within organizations. To advance this important work, organizations need to address some specific topics. We can see how some companies have opted to tread lightly with respect to key issues—or not address them at all. With uncharted territory, it can be difficult to be a pioneer in both goals and solutions. However, if organizations are not addressing these issues, it may mean that they are leaving people behind.

The main imperative in the here and now is retaining people and making sure the environments created for employees are supportive, inclusive, equitable, and accessible. From that place of belonging, creative solutions and effective approaches are born. All of this supports modeling of a world that we can live and thrive in—that can impact society as a whole. Let's look at how the forces present today have disrupted what is status quo around ERGs and DEI in the workplace in general and have made us envision a new future.

In not-so-distant times, the business case for employee resource groups—as presented to and adopted by executive leaders—focused on what ERGs could provide to the company in a direct way, related to company objectives. Demonstrating how general DEI initiatives drove the business bottom line in terms of marketplace reach or product innovation was sometimes the way that these efforts could get support and traction. However, with the widespread stresses of the pandemic, racial unrest in society, the recent "Great Resignation," the global shift in attitude toward work and office environments, and the focus on advancing one's own pursuits and needs in the context of self-care and intentional living, the tables have not only turned but have completely flipped over. Professionals in the workplace, who now have more options, are seeking more valuable experiences of employment and therefore hold more power in their demands for workplaces that demonstrate equity, opportunity, and environments free from bias and microaggressions.

These items have always been on the wish list for many people of marginalized identities and allies, and organizations are wholeheartedly committing to them, but leadership now has the urgency of public outcry, *plus* the competitive market for talent, to deliver these outcomes *quickly*. Of course, you could make the case that supporting people *is* the way to support the bottom line. To be effective, organizations must be able to maintain operations through change and transition and retain their workforce. At the same time, we have seen a noticeable shift in that the priority for employees is less about making companies money, the commerce part of the equation, and more about creating places of community and an enjoyable career. What people really want to know and feel is that their organizations *care*.

Frankly, there is a large swath of people who just want to be happy and have a good quality of life at work, rather than solely focusing on moving ahead. If they don't have that, they will readily choose to leave. This shift is palpable. ERGs are the instruments of engagement that can help sustain and fulfill the workforce during times of challenge, change, and a deprioritizing of working. In essence, work shouldn't feel like work. The movement to have offices that offer food, transportation, places to exercise, and places to physically gather for community events was *life* integrating into *work*. The pendulum has swung the other way, where *work* now has to fit into *life*. Work has become an extension of life. And for employees, engaging in it is now more of a choice.

The key behind the success of an organization, then, is this: truly creating cultures of belonging and inclusion for all of its people and helping to reduce barriers for individuals from groups that have been historically excluded or systematically oppressed. Truly effective leadership embodies the full support of employees who have gone through the stressful experiences of a global pandemic, racial and political unrest, and the tragic loss of loved ones. The transformational change needed is to create organizational environments where people not only work but can exist freely and wholly, without the shame or exclusion of difference and suppression of talent due to bias. The ultimate goal is surfacing the true potential of each person. When that happens, the possibilities for both the employee and the company are endless.

What this concretely looks like is gender and racial parity in leadership roles, pay equity, retention of people with marginalized identities, trauma-informed programming, accessible resources, increased autonomy in the workplace, and support for mental health and general wellness and healing. In order to compete in today's market, organizations must leapfrog into new versions of themselves that were imagined in a slower and conceptual way. What is being called for now is the immediate and actionable. With people leaving organizations for better positions, or leaving the workforce in general due to their own choice or circumstances limiting their participation (such as a lack of childcare options), this transformational experience of work is overdue. *We are all out of time.*

The plot twist in this ending of the book is that the future is actually *now*. It is not something we have the luxury of visualizing in a long-term idealized state. We are crouched in it, huddling to make decisions, and are actively creating it as each day goes by. It is here, it is urgent, and it needs us to take hold of the reins and fearlessly steer it. People in the workplace are out of patience, resources, focus, and the wherewithal to wait for an idealized experience of work that is promised much later. They want to see it in the present, today.

In order for leaders to carve out what is next, they must readily acknowledge both the past and the current state of affairs that may still need much of our attention. What matters to employees and leaders at your organization? The first step is listening to hear what matters are top of mind, and the second step is to take action to address and alleviate some of those issues. They include sensitive topics that organizations are hesitant to address. In my consulting work, I have identified key areas that leadership within organizations should focus on, in order to be current and also responsive to the needs of their employees and other stakeholders. There are many more, but here are just a few of those issues. Consider how some of these areas show up at your organization, as well as other issues that should be addressed.

INDIGENOUS COMMUNITIES

How do you involve Indigenous employees at your organization? Do you have an ERG for these communities that is separate from other groups, or are they combined with others? How do you engage with the greater public and the Indigenous communities where your office buildings are located or where you live? Addressing the needs of individuals identifying as Native American, First Nations, Alaskan Native, Native Hawaiian, or Pacific Islander, and of other Indigenous community groups in your region, is of utmost importance. A space for Indigenous individuals to gather and build together as a community would be significant, even if you have a small number of employees who identify in this way. Due to the problematic history and systemic exclusion of First Peoples in many countries, it is critical that there be an intention to create space and include employees of Indigenous backgrounds, as well as to connect to Indigenous communities in your area, outside of your organization. However, properly establishing awareness and relations among these communities takes effort and education. We must not shy away from this.

I have consulted to companies where there has been tremendous pushback against doing a land acknowledgment (verbal honoring of the Indigenous peoples and meaningful connection to the land where you are located) to start a particular event, because there had been no previous relationship between the workplace and the local Indigenous community or public recognition of the historical relations among various groups. On the other hand, some organizations are yearning to learn more about how to incorporate Indigenous land acknowledgments into events like their fundraising galas, groundbreakings, or tours of building facilities. What is the reaction toward land acknowledgments at your own organization? Is there still a need to grow awareness about them and also how to introduce them appropriately? How can you have a deeper conversation about the inclusion of First Peoples, beyond these types of acknowledgments, continuing forward?

In contrast to these examples, in my time in Hawai'i and in parts of Canada, I witnessed various institutions having it be a norm and part of their culture to honor and acknowledge local Indigenous communities and the historical and current relationships with First Peoples. The reluctance of some other organizations to be involved with this can be traced to the painful history of genocide and treatment of Indigenous peoples in many regions, which can cause alarm, guilt, and shame among those from dominant identities or a fear of making a mistake. However, the lack of action can communicate a lack of concern for these communities, even if unintended.

At the time of this writing, there had been the significant news of the discovery of thousands of bodies of Native residential school children in Canada who were killed and buried on the premises of these schools. The horrific treatment and ongoing trauma experienced by Indigenous communities is challenging to know and witness. Companies responded to these events with varying degrees of engagement. At the same time, there is also a living Indigenous community that is strong in culture and ties to values that should be recognized and supported in the workplace, not solely defined by tragedy but celebrated for its fullness and richness on its own. Engaging with Native-owned businesses and community groups could be a proactive endeavor for leaders and your company. What else can you initiate or do? Establishing a connection with First Peoples of the lands that a company inhabits is foundational to all other efforts.

To take the conversation further, how are Indigenous groups recognized and categorized at your company? Asian American and Pacific Islander communities are usually brought together under the banner of the AAPI community. However, employees at some companies have told me that Native Hawaiian and Pacific Islander communities may feel more connection to Native American ERGs due to the common experiences of being of Indigenous backgrounds. Leaders in organizations should recognize this and foster open dialogue with community members about how to organize the ERGs so that the employees of these communities are best supported. Members of all ERGs should endeavor to understand the perspectives of Native community members and support how they wish to participate and organize.

Indigenous communities need to be recognized and supported and their culture not be commodified. As with any ERG—in particular, ERGs of Native communities—it is important to consult leaders of the ERGs if an idea or larger action is being planned for the organization (such as a campaign by the small business Eighth Generation to market products with a Native-inspired design)[1] that may create a response by Indigenous group members (for instance, a movement to engage Native artists). The ongoing dialogue is key for the support of Indigenous community members, and it can create opportunities for true engagement and community building through awareness and participation. The potential opportunity here is to rebuild ties and grow relations among Indigenous communities, as well as connection to their causes through intentional inclusion and collaboration. How will your organization embark upon this?

The Indigenous community is an example of a community where there is an opportunity for growth, connection, and greater representation and belonging in the workplace. What other groups at your organization could benefit from ongoing support and a concerted effort toward inclusion, equity, and access? How is the Black community supported and celebrated at your workplace, through events, actions, and communication? How is the Latinx community honored and served at your organization in a culturally responsive and inclusive way? What about veterans or families of those in the military? Or people with neurodiversity as a prevalent identity? It is critical to understand what groups within your organization may benefit from the support of an employee resource group and then to have a plan for initiating and continuing that support. At the same time, these demographics are constantly changing. How can you address this dynamic as well?

EMERGING AND GROWING DEMOGRAPHICS

Companies can succeed at cultivating belonging at their workplace by acknowledging and addressing the changing and existing workforce demographics. Most companies have employee resource groups for demographics related to race, gender, sexual orientation, age, military background, and parental status. But what about employees who do not fit neatly in those categories set up in your existing framework? Or who strongly belong to more than one group at the same time? Leadership within organizations must be prepared to flex and be responsive to growing populations and demographics that may surface as employee presence and voices from these groups grow. How does your organization support multiracial individuals and transracial adoptees? Or address religious affiliations and observances? How can you informally support employees who are immigrants and on work visas? What about individuals who live an intersectional identity and may not feel they belong to ERGs as they are organized now?

An example comes from the multiracial community, which I am very much involved with, given my work, research, and authorship on this topic.[2] Recent United States Census data indicates an increase in people who identify as multiracial from 9 million people to 33.8 million people, an increase of 276 percent. This is partly due to how the data was gathered and also due to the overall growing acceptance and awareness about this identity as an option and now acceptable reality for many people. The newly formed Mixed Googlers ERG and the multiracial ERG forming at McKinsey are two terrific examples of the emerging demographics of working professionals who identify as biracial and multiracial, or multiethnic. These companies are actively supporting their employees who identify as mixed race or have multiracial children, but such cases are few, and there need to be more groups meeting this need.

The hope is that more and more companies will address this population and will set aside resources and prioritization of these groups. Multiracial people have specific experiences, and the needs they express to have their own space in which to participate and process are crucial in creating an inclusive company culture. Similarly, the experience of transracial adoptees is unique and may not fit into a monoracial and monolithic conception of race that existing ERGs may be modeled after.

The task at hand is to explore how to support individuals who may not be fully represented by the existing ERGs, as they are part of a specific population within existing ERGs that isn't highlighted, due to having an intersectional identity. For example, how do you support someone who identifies as Two Spirit (non-binary and Indigenous) if the existing structures in the Pride group don't include 2S in the acronym (that is, LGBTQIA2S+), and then individuals face unintentional exclusion? Although many employee resource groups may not yet do the same, Netflix's Pride@ ERG utilizes the LGBTQIA2S+ acronym to describe members of their group, undoubtedly extending the experience of belonging and communicating the importance of inclusion to a wider range of people. The work to address the many layers of identity continues and should be an effort that all ERG and organizational leaders try to explore and address further, by cocreating new spaces and also making sure that existing spaces are mindful of the identities that are being held and supported. Awareness about a community stemming from ERG participation that informs action and inclusive communication demonstrates how the presence of these groups is truly honoring the intersectionality and breadth and depth of identities that can be found at each organization.

ENGAGING ALLIES

Allyship is a key to the success of the creation of an inclusive organizational culture. Cross-ERG collaboration is an effective way to cultivate a deeper sense of allyship and engagement, including those who may not belong to the particular ERG demographic. As the general DEI consciousness within companies rises and is reinforced through self-awareness, training, coaching, and organizational commitments, what comes next is to identify what to do when we discover bias in ourselves or those around us, and inequity in the systems we work with. Allies can be the messengers and activators around policies and approaches that need to change in order to create more inclusive environments for others.

ERGs can facilitate the engagement of allies within any existing group, and organizations can start an ERG dedicated to allyship for all groups. One company I work with has an allyship group named Allyship for All, a fantastic gathering of enthusiastic individuals committed to showing up in the workplace for the cause of supporting others and creating pathways for underrepresented individuals to join the industry and company. These examples show how ERGs can create a place for people of dominant identities to play a role in DEI initiatives, in an authentic rather than performative way.

ECONOMIC WELL-BEING

How else has the world of work, as we have known it, been disrupted? The consequences of the COVID-19 pandemic, coupled with ongoing systemic inequity with regard to pay and economic opportunity, have created a very deep need to support individuals financially. Employees are making the calculation of whether going to work is feasible and worth it. Parents and caregivers of children are facing financial constraints or shortages of childcare options. Individuals who have lost loved ones or who have medical bills have to deal with limited monthly income due to increased expenses. People who are immunocompromised may be unable to return to work as office buildings open and employees go back to meeting in person. The gap widens between those who have privilege and those who don't. How can companies support their employees and mitigate the risks of losing valuable employees due to the constraints of the times?

There is a rapidly growing need for an increase in financial education and other resources for supporting the financial health of employees that companies should consider providing. These resources and offerings are attractive to both potential and current employees, and they also indicate a culture of care that is important to those in the workplace today. The key for employee resource group leaders is to deliver the information to ERG members in a culturally sensitive and accessible way.

One example of financial literacy education that is geared toward BIPOC communities is the podcast and financial education platform *Earn Your Leisure*.[3] This podcast, hosted by Rashad Bilal and Troy Millings, has become a global phenomenon because it has penetrated BIPOC and in particular Black communities around the world, offering content that is free, accessible, and inspiring. As a guest on this top-ranked podcast speaking about small business resources for minority entrepreneurs and supplier diversity opportunities, I have witnessed firsthand how both the delivery of the information and the encouraging approach of the hosts are extremely motivational for members of the community.[4]

Companies that engage speakers and content that is targeted toward their ERG members and community partners can have highly successful results in the attendance of events, absorption of information, and adoption of new habits that can help the economic well-being of employees from underrepresented and historically marginalized communities. As a result, organizations that support an employee's overall financial wellness will be fostering loyalty and connection among their staff and community partners in a legitimate way that can create immense impact in an individual's household and affect generations to come.

MENTAL HEALTH

How has your organization addressed the issue of mental health in the workplace? Do you have a sense of how it is valued by your employees? If not, conducting a survey or checking in with your ERG members would be a good way to ascertain the impact of mental health on employees' sense of satisfaction in the workplace and even their performance. When the city of Columbus, Ohio, Human Resources Conference team sent a poll to its members about topics of interest for an upcoming conference, the top-ranked issue was mental health. This is not surprising, given the struggles that many of us have faced due to the limitations of the pandemic, the experience of challenging racial and political events, economic pressures, loss and sickness of loved ones, caregiving of children and elders, schooling and working at home, and the resulting physical and mental toll that all of these variables have taken on all of us. To expand on what was mentioned previously, companies that have employee assistance programs (EAPs) can leverage ERGs to help disseminate information about these programs and destigmatize conceptions about seeking help for mental health.

At the same time, the existing models of mental health can be supplemented with additional forms of healing that are common in culturally diverse communities. In my consulting practice, I engage healer facilitators to support organizational clients providing energetic healing sessions for employees. These sessions involve guided meditations, discussion, and calming energetic release activities geared toward the cultural community at hand. Such activities are helpful in supporting the calming of the collective organizational nervous system and the releasing of energetic charge and emotions that have built up over time. Healing work is essential for any DEI strategy to take hold, and it must be done in a trauma-informed way with psychological safety and cultural sensitivity at the forefront of any engagement.

ERGs are the conduits of these gatherings, and they are also the source of feedback to organizational and HR leadership when employees who are ERG members share freely in confidence what their challenges are and what some solutions and responses could be. This safe and responsive means of retrieving feedback and engaging in support for employees has made ERGs one of the most needed components of an organization. Without ERGs, many employees would not have the support they need to get through the day and successfully do their jobs.

These are just a few of the issues that organizations should think about addressing—and there certainly are many more. The key approach that cannot be overstated is the need for leaders to listen to employees and take note of what employee resource groups raise in terms of concerns or areas of attention. We must not fear what is surfaced through ERGs and instead should welcome the feedback, as it comes from a place of earnest commitment, care, and dedication to the organization's purpose and role. It also will save organizations from the dread of embarrassment or oversight, as ERGs are a microcosm of the society that surrounds us, and they can share valuable input to make services, products, and overall company functioning even better.

This is the power of employee resource groups—that they are the collective voice for people who may not always be seen or heard as individuals. Due to systemic bias and historical exclusion of underserved communities, individuals who are underrepresented can turn to employee resource groups as safe and often comfortable corners in the workplace that may be vastly different from what is found in the general daily workings of one's job because they center the needs and experiences of the identity that is usually marginalized and put it in the spotlight in an inclusive and supportive way. People can simply *belong* more easily in those spaces.

Organizations should understand and appreciate that ERGs represent the gathering of individuals who may be smaller in number than in the general population—yet whose voices matter and should be listened to and engaged sensitively and consistently. ERGs need to be supported by organizations and understood as essential mechanisms for communication, collaboration, and actions that go beyond a reaction to a single current news item or fad or trend. This is how organizational efforts can be made sustainable and kept up in an ongoing way. The power of employee resource groups is also in the tremendous effect they can have within a company, which we can witness in the framework of the many pillars they operate in and even beyond. The impact that ERGs can have on any organization is vast and far-reaching, and it can impact society as a whole.

As we discussed at the beginning of this book with the Trifecta of Organizational Change™ model, true organizational transformation cannot occur without the engagement of key stakeholders, including the public, leadership, and the employees themselves. ERGs represent a large group of the workforce who can also lead out an effort. Employee resource groups can support organizations in any course that is charted, any effort that is initiated, and can do so naturally and authentically. ERGs have had a finger on the pulse of how people feel, both within and outside of the organization, and are major influencers and conveyors of culture.

Organizations need ERGs and at the same time can guide them toward a larger goal and objective that is aligned with the company's vision for inclusion, equity, belonging, and access. These are the ingredients for a positive workplace environment, and they are a large part of the recipe for effective, healthy, and successful organizations.

My hope is that this book has expanded your awareness of the power, possibilities, and potential of employee resource groups. Whatever your organization's stage along the journey of diversity, equity, and inclusion, consider ERGs to be a valuable asset for supporting employees, company goals, and overall society through an inclusive and equitable workplace environment. Initiating discussions about starting an ERG or supporting ones that currently exist strongly signals your dedication to people at your organization. In these continuing moments of great uncertainty, this commitment will get us through.

As you carry on with your journey, you will continue to experience the tremendous power and impact of employee resource groups. I look forward to seeing how you and your colleagues lead the authentic change that is needed in our world, now and into the future.

· GLOSSARY ·

ADVOCACY—Support for a cause, policy, or group.

AFFINITY GROUP—A group of people having a common interest or goal or acting together for a specific purpose. In institutional settings, this is a group that gathers and organizes around a common demographic characteristic such as race, gender, or other identity trait, in order to create community.

ALLY (PL. *ALLIES*)—Someone who makes the commitment and effort to recognize their privilege (based on gender, class, race, sexual identity, etc.) and work in solidarity with oppressed groups in efforts toward equity, inclusion, and justice. Allies understand that it is in their own interest to end all forms of oppression, even those from which they may benefit in concrete ways. Allies commit to reducing their own complicity or collusion in oppression of those groups and invest in strengthening their own knowledge and awareness of oppression.

ALLYSHIP—The practice of being an ally. (See *ally*.)

BACKER—A person in the DEI Stakeholder Disposition framework described as responsive and actively in support of DEI initiatives at an organization.

BELONGING—A sense of fitting in, acceptance, comfort, and inclusion, as a member of a particular identity or group.

BIPOC—Acronym for Black, Indigenous, and people of color that emphasizes authentic and lasting solidarity among these groups while highlighting the particular experiences of Indigenous and Black people, in order to undo Native invisibility and anti-Blackness.

BUSINESS RESOURCE GROUPS (BRGS)—Employee-led groups that gather people of shared identities in the workplace with a focus on connecting to business objectives and company goals. (See *employee resource groups*.)

CHALLENGER SAFETY—Condition where an individual has the ability to challenge the status quo of an environment in good faith and with candor. This provides the space for innovation within organizations.

CODE-SWITCHING—Originally referring to switching across languages, code-switching refers to an individual's adaptation of behavior, manner of speaking, physical appearance, and other characteristics to match those of people or situations around them.

CORPORATE SOCIAL RESPONSIBILITY (CSR)—The prioritization of social and environmental concerns into organizational leadership, strategy, practices, and policies.

DEI STAKEHOLDER DISPOSITION—A framework that describes individuals on the axes of being active and in support, or not active and unsupportive, of DEI initiatives at an organization.

DIVERSITY—Diversity includes all the ways in which people differ, and it encompasses all the different characteristics that make one individual or group different from one another. It is all-inclusive and recognizes that everyone should be valued. A broad definition includes not only race, ethnicity, and gender—the groups that most often come to mind when the term *diversity* is used—but also age, national origin, religion, disability, sexual orientation, socioeconomic status, education, marital status, parental or caregiver status, language, and physical appearance. It involves different ideas, perspectives, and values as well.

DIVERSITY COUNCIL—A group of individuals of different backgrounds at an organization, usually senior leaders or executives, that lead organizations toward diversity, equity, and inclusion goals.

DIVERSITY, EQUITY, AND INCLUSION (DEI)—Policies, programs, and strategy that promote the representation, participation, and belonging of members of different identity groups and demographics at an organization. (See *diversity*.)

EMPLOYEE RESOURCE GROUP (ERG)—A group of employees created at a workplace with a defined purpose and an organizational process, and organized around and in service of a particular demographic category or identity characteristic.

EQUITY—Acknowledgment, treatment, actions, and opportunity to address the fact that many groups in society have not always been given equal treatment and are frequently made to feel inferior and oppressed. This can be in the form of education, awareness building around specific issues, and special programs and benefits for those who have been discriminated against and are in need of opportunity.

HISTORICALLY EXCLUDED—Any group of people that has been denied access to full rights, privileges, and opportunities in a society or organization.

INCLUSION—Authentically bringing traditionally excluded individuals and/or groups into processes, activities, decision-making, and policy making in a way that shares power.

INCLUSION COUNCIL—A gathering of individuals from a cross-section of demographics within an organization with the intention and purpose of cultivating inclusion and equity in the workplace environment.

INCLUSION SAFETY—Condition whereby an individual has the ability to be included and interact in an environment without the presence of harm.

INEQUITY—The experience and understanding that many groups in society have not always been given equal treatment and are frequently made to feel inferior and oppressed.

INTERSECTIONALITY—An approach largely advanced by women of color and coined and documented by Kimberlé Crenshaw, stating that classifications such as gender, race, and class cannot be examined in isolation from one another and can result in compounded oppression. The classifications interact and intersect in individuals' lives, in society, and in social systems.

LATENT ALLY—A person in the DEI Stakeholder Composition framework described as a less responsive supporter of DEI initiatives at an organization.

MARGINALIZATION—Treatment of a person, group, or concept as insignificant or peripheral; relegation to an unimportant or powerless position within a society or group.

MARGINALIZED—A person who experiences marginalization. (See *marginalization*.)

NON-BINARY IDENTITY—Identity that cannot be defined within the gender binary of male and female.

OBSTRUCTIONIST—A person in the DEI Stakeholder Composition framework described as actively not supportive of DEI initiatives at an organization.

OTHERING—Treating someone differently or excluding from a social group.

POTENTIAL SUPPORTER—A person in the DEI Stakeholder Composition framework who may be in support of DEI initiatives at an organization.

PSYCHOLOGICAL SAFETY—A condition where people feel included, safe to learn, safe to contribute, and safe to challenge the status quo. The presence of psychological safety allows for interaction, learning, and open exchange, and it invites innovation in organizations.

RACE—There is no biological basis for racial categories, and genetic research has shown more within-group variations than between-group variations. Races are socially and politically constructed categories that others have assigned on the basis of physical characteristics, such as skin color or hair type. Although race is a social construction, the impact of race is real, as perceptions of race influence our beliefs, stereotypes, economic opportunities, and everyday experiences.

SURVIVORSHIP BIAS—A type of selection bias where the focus is on successful instances and individuals rather than the failures of those who are not present, due to a lack of visibility. This bias can lead to false conclusions and beliefs.

SYSTEMIC OPPRESSION—Systemic devaluing, undermining, marginalizing, and disadvantaging of certain social identities in contrast to the privileged norm: when some people are denied something of value, while others have ready access.

TOXIC POSITIVITY—The belief or assumption that people should maintain a positive outlook regardless of how challenging or tragic a situation is.

TRIFECTA OF ORGANIZATIONAL CHANGE™—A triangular model of transformational change consisting of the key stakeholders of leadership, employees, and the public. This model demonstrates how movement toward organizational transformation can occur when each key stakeholder is engaged and participating in the process.

UNCONSCIOUS BIAS (ALSO KNOWN AS IMPLICIT BIAS)—Negative associations that people unknowingly hold. They are expressed automatically, without conscious awareness, and affect individuals' attitudes, actions, and behaviors.

UNDERREPRESENTED—A person or thing that is inadequately represented within a group, an organization, or general society.

· NOTES ·

Chapter 1

1. Judi C. Casey, "Employee Resource Groups: A Strategic Business Resource for Today's Workplace," Boston College Center for Work & Family, https://www.bc.edu/content/dam/files/centers/cwf/research/publications3 /executivebriefingseries-2/ExecutiveBriefing_EmployeeResourceGroups.pdf (accessed September 14, 2021).
2. Theresa M. Welbourne, Skylar Rolf, Steven Schlachter, "The Case for Employee Resource Groups: A Review and Social Identity Theory-Based Research Agenda," Center for Effective Organizations, November 2016, https://ceo.usc.edu/wp-content/uploads/2019/07/G16-10677.pdf (accessed February 21, 2021).
3. Welbourne et al., "The Case for Employee Resource Groups."
4. Jeff Green, "Deloitte Thinks Diversity Groups are Passé," *Bloomberg*, July 19, 2017, https://www.bloomberg.com/news/articles/2017-07-19/deloitte -thinks-diversity-groups-are-pass (accessed December 3, 2021).
5. Barbara Frankel and Karen Dahms, *ERG Leadership Handbook* (Diversity Best Practices, 2019).

Chapter 2

1. Frank Dobbin and Alexandra Kalev, "Why Diversity Programs Fail," *Harvard Business Review*, July–August, 2016, https://hbr.org/2016/07 /why-diversity-programs-fail (accessed March 2, 2021).
2. Sara Frueh, "Making Diversity Programs More Effective," *National Academies of Sciences, Engineering, Medicine*, May 7, 2020, https:// www.nationalacademies.org/news/2020/05/making-diversity-programs -more-effective (accessed May 15, 2021).
3. Edward H. Chang et al., "Does Diversity Training Work the Way It's Supposed To?" *Harvard Business Review*, July 9, 2019, https://hbr .org/2019/07/does-diversity-training-work-the-way-its-supposed-to (accessed March 14, 2021).
4. Edward H. Chang et al., "The Mixed Effects of Online Diversity Training," *Proceedings of the National Academy of Sciences of the United States of America*, April 16, 2019, https://www.pnas.org/content/116/16/7778 (accessed April 20, 2021).

5. Vivian Hunt, DBE, et al., *Diversity Wins: How Inclusion Matters*, McKinsey & Company, May 2020, https://www.mckinsey.com/~/media/mckinsey /featured%20insights/diversity%20and%20inclusion/diversity%20wins%20 how%20inclusion%20matters/diversity-wins-how-inclusion-matters-vf .pdf?shouldIndex=false (accessed April 20, 2020).

6. Mike Isaac, "What You Need to Know About #DeleteUber," *New York Times*, January 31, 2017, https://www.nytimes.com/2017/01/31/business /delete-uber.html (accessed May 15, 2021).

7. Susan Fowler, "Reflecting on One Very, Very Strange Year at Uber," *Susan Fowler*, February 19, 2017, https://www.susanjfowler.com/blog/2017/2/19 /reflecting-on-one-very-strange-year-at-uber (accessed June 10, 2021).

8. Forum on Workplace Inclusion, "What We Do Next Matters Most: Case Studies of Crisis, Resilience, Inclusion, and Belonging at Uber and Unilever," YouTube, June 8, 2018, https://www.youtube.com/watch?v=E3xMkTf3Jso (accessed April 16, 2021).

Chapter 3

1. Sheryl Estrada, "Twitter to Pay Resource Group Leaders, Saying the Work Shouldn't Be a 'Volunteer Activity,'" *HR Dive*, October 6, 2020, https:// www.hrdive.com/news/twitter-to-pay-resource-group-leaders-saying-the -work-shouldnt-be-a-volu/586489/ (accessed February 10, 2021).

2. Rachel Montañez, "LinkedIn Is Now Paying ERG Leaders; This Is Huge in the Battle Against Burnout," *Forbes*, June 3, 2021, https://www.forbes.com /sites/rachelmontanez/2021/06/03/linkedin-is-now-paying-erg-leaders-this -is-huge-in-the-battle-against-burnout/?sh=421f01e82ab7 (accessed July 5, 2021).

3. Hope King, "Exclusive: LinkedIn to Pay Its ERG leaders," *Axios*, June 2, 2021, https://www.axios.com/linkedin-erg-pay-affinity-groups-17b9a060 -0ef3-4226-aae2-a3dbe56908f9.html (accessed August 30, 2021).

4. Jes Osrow, "2020 Report: Are You Paying Your ERG Leads?" Rise Journey, April 6, 2021, https://www.therisejourney.com/we-rise-a-blog/are-you -paying-your-erg-leads (accessed July 25, 2021).

5. Dalana Brand, "Inclusion & Diversity Report July 2021: Cultivating Inclusion," Twitter Blog, July 15, 2021, https://blog.twitter.com/en_us /topics/company/2021/inclusion-and-diversity-report-cultivating-inclusion -july-2021 (accessed August 13, 2021).

6. Sheryl Estrada, "Twitter to Pay Resource Group Leaders, Saying the Work Shouldn't Be a 'Volunteer Activity,'" *HR Dive*, October 6, 2020, https:// www.hrdive.com/news/twitter-to-pay-resource-group-leaders-saying-the -work-shouldnt-be-a-volu/586489/ (accessed November 5, 2021).

Chapter 5

1. Jennifer Brown, *Inclusion: Diversity, the New Workplace & the Will to Change* (Hartford, CT: Publish Your Purpose Press, 2017).

2. Jennifer Brown Consulting, "Employee Resource Groups That Drive Business," https://jenniferbrownconsulting.com/wp-content/uploads/2020/05/1-Employee-Resource-Groups.pdf (accessed June 12, 2021).

3. Edward E. Hubbard and Myra K. Hubbard, *Measuring the ROI Impact of ERGs and BRGs: Ensuring Employee Resource Group Initiatives Drive Business and Organizational Results*, 1st ed. (Petaluma, CA: Global Insights Publishing, 2013).

Chapter 6

1. Aiko Bethea, "What Black Employee Resource Groups Need Right Now," *Harvard Business Review*, June 29, 2020, https://hbr.org/2020/06/what-black-employee-resource-groups-need-right-now (accessed May 20, 2021).

Chapter 8

1. Erby L. Foster, email message to author, December 5, 2021.

2. Hallmark, *Hallmark Diversity & Inclusion: Walgreens Store in San Francisco's Castro Neighborhood*, YouTube, March 15, 2016, https://www.youtube.com/watch?v=qVoEL09CywU (accessed August 14, 2021).

3. Michael Gonzales, email message to author, December 6, 2021.

4. Jimmy Hua, email message to author, December 5, 2021.

5. Mara Santilli, "A Bright Spot," *Marie Claire*, Winter 2020, 46.

6. Erby L. Foster, email message to author, December 5, 2021.

Chapter 9

1. Natasha Brennan, "Eighth Generation Founder Weaves Heritage and Healing to Reclaim Space for Native Art," *News Tribune*, November 26, 2021, https://www.thenewstribune.com/news/state/washington/article256110632.html (accessed December 8, 2021).

2. Farzana Nayani, *Raising Multiracial Children: Tools for Nurturing Identity in a Racialized World* (Berkeley, CA: North Atlantic Books, 2020).

3. *Earn Your Leisure*, https://www.earnyourleisure.com/pages/our-story (accessed November 30, 2021).

4. "Corporate and Business Programs," *Earn Your Leisure*, Episode 77, YouTube, https://www.youtube.com/watch?v=HC_U_konh3U (accessed February 14, 2021).

· RESOURCES ·

Further Reading

Brown, Jennifer. *Inclusion: Diversity, the New Workplace & the Will to Change*. Hartford, CT: Publish Your Purpose Press, 2016.

Frankel, Barbara, and Karen Dahms. *ERG Leadership Handbook* (Seramount [formerly Diversity Best Practices]).

Hubbard, Edward E., and Myra K. Hubbard. *Measuring the ROI Impact of ERGs and BRGs: Ensuring Employee Resource Group Initiatives Drive Business and Organizational Results*, 1st ed. Global Insights Publishing, 2013.

Rodriguez, Robert. *Employee Resource Group Excellence: Grow High Performing ERGs to Enhance Diversity, Equality, Belonging, and Business Impact*. Hoboken, NJ: John Wiley & Sons, 2021.

Welbourne, Theresa M., Skylar Rolf, and Steven Schlachter. "Employee Resource Groups: An Introduction, Review and Research Agenda." *Academy of Management Proceedings* 2015, no. 1.

ERG Educational Events and Conferences

Diversity Advocates, https://diversityadvocates.com; Our Collective, https://ourcollective.us

Diversity Woman Media Conferences, https://www.diversitywoman.com/our-conferences/

Elevate National ERG Summit & Leadership Forum, http://www.ergsummit.com/

EmERGe Leadership Summit, https://seramount.com/events-conferences/conferences/emerge-leadership-summit

ERG & Council Conference, https://www.ergcouncilconference.com/

Forum on Workplace Inclusion, https://forumworkplaceinclusion.org

Kapor Center, https://www.kaporcenter.org

Mogul International ERG Day, https://onmogul.com/internationalergday

National Diversity and Leadership Conference, http://nationaldiversityconference.com/2020/

USC Marshall Center for Effective Organizations, https://ceo.usc.edu

· ACKNOWLEDGMENTS ·

I open these acknowledgments honoring the Tongva peoples on whose land I currently reside and where most of this book was written, the xwməθkwəy̓əm (Musqueam) and all Coast Salish peoples upon whose land I was raised, and the Kānaka ʻōiwi or Kānaka maoli of the islands of Hawaiʻi whose ʻaina (land) I had settled on, as it is within all of these places that I have formed much of my existence and the perspectives that I share here. I also acknowledge the ancestors from these communities as well as other communities I have been a part of and in contact with, who have offered guidance, support, and direction for this project and my work overall.

This book is dedicated to all who are devoted to advancing inclusion, belonging, and understanding within the workplaces we occupy and thrive in. The current times have been challenging, and the insights shared by those who are on the frontlines doing this work are incredibly inspiring to me. Although I may not mention your names to preserve your confidentiality, I hold your stories sacred, and as I share them in this book, know that they do provide enlightenment and healing to others.

I have many people to thank for the creation of this book. Appreciation to my editor Neal Maillet and the entire team at my publisher, Berrett-Koehler, who had the foresight to reach out to me to write this book and who came together with a unified effort, despite all odds, to create a pathway for this book's message to reach the world. Alongside my publisher, I acknowledge my other colleagues in the publishing industry who offered ongoing support throughout the process. A gracious thank-you to the clients and partnering organizations whom I have worked with over the years and who have become friends, for opening their doors to the experiment and intentionality of effort that diversity, equity, and inclusion strategy and action truly is. Gratitude to my consulting team: Emi Lea Kamemoto, Alma Ramos, Leah Domantay, Sean Oliver, Keith Nishida, Diyana Mendoza-Price, Sophie-Claire Kanno, Justin Sitron,

Miriam Khalifa, and Taikera Conyers, for your support. You have been the backbone of my work and have tendered so much in the form of contribution and heart to create impact and organizational transformational change. I appreciate you all. A huge embrace to the WAYFINDERS, DEI Explorers, DEI Navigators, and community at Multiracial Matters™ who have chosen to spend seasons with me to learn, grow, and pass on the collective learning. Humble admiration to my trusted advisors, mentors, friends, and colleagues in the field, notably Erby L. Foster; Murray Mann; Michael Gonzales; Jimmy Hua; Mohammed Farshori; Mary Farmer; Noah Balch; Sherry Wallen; Susan Deland; 10KSB scholars, faculty, and organizers; Benedict Tubuo; Farhan Manjiyani; Anam Virani; Christina Dedios; Lisa Strack; Rahimeh Ramezany; Shaiyanne Dar; and Charles Babb: your feedback and ability to see and guide me with protection and care has been tantamount to any success I have had. To the healers who have the ability to put things back together that are broken and shine light where it is needed: Anisa Kassim, Ramona Laughing Brook Webb, Malia Wright, Malliha Ahmad, Essence, Anna Salumbides, Anushah Jiwani, Dr. Jennifer Lisa Vest, and Katrina Long. Eternal love to my family, especially to my children, Zakri and Zain, and my husband, Shafiq, who have been essential to my survival in the depths of this work and are the continued inspiration for my commitment to the vision of making the world a better place. You are the sunshine, joy, and nourishment in my life.

This book is an opening to deepen the conversation about how to support underrepresented and historically marginalized groups within our organizations and society overall—and with that, what transformational change can occur. We are seeing rapid growth in this work, and at the same time, much of it is uncharted, as there is so much more to go. To all the readers who have embarked on this journey and who I see as leaders: this book is dedicated to *you*. May you continue to find the tools, confidence, and wherewithal to continue the task at hand: uplifting the identities of ourselves and those around us, and cultivating equity, access, and belonging for all.

·INDEX·

trust, 13, 88
Twitter, 40–41, 43
Two Spirit (nonbinary and
    Indigenous), 120–21

U

Uber, 23–25, 27
unconscious bias (implicit bias), 59,
    130
underrepresented communities, 5, 130.
    See also identities, nondominant
University of Colorado Denver, 87–88

V

vision and mission, 33–34, 35
volunteering, 70–71

W

Wayfair employee coalition, 23
wellness rooms, 86
"What We Do Next Matters Most:
    Case Studies of Crisis, Resilience,
    Inclusion, and Belonging at Uber
    and Unilever," 24

White House, 109
White-identified employees, 87, 89–90
White leaders, 8, 47–48, 89–90
Wilson, Joseph, 3
workforce, 65, 66–68, 73
    demographics, 119–21
    global, 95, 96–98, 100
workplace, 65, 68–69, 73

X

Xenophobia, 84
Xerox
    National Black Employee Caucus, 3

Z

Zomato (food-delivery start-up), 110

· ABOUT THE AUTHOR ·

Farzana Nayani
Diversity, Equity, and
Inclusion Consultant;
Author; Executive Coach

FARZANA NAYANI (she/hers) is a recognized diversity, equity, and inclusion specialist, coach, and international keynote speaker. She has worked with Fortune 500 corporations, public agencies, higher education institutions, school districts, and non-profit organizations as a consultant and trainer on diversity and inclusion, intercultural communication, supplier diversity, and employee engagement.

Farzana's advisory work with employee resource groups (ERGs), small business advocacy, and entrepreneurship has taken her to engagements across North America, from the White House to Silicon Valley. Her subject matter expertise on global community relations is recognized in her work with such institutions as the Smithsonian Institution and the East-West Center. She is currently an advisor to the Asian Leaders Alliance and is the former National Director of ERG relations for the National Association of Asian American Professionals. Farzana's expertise has been featured in media outlets such as the *Wall Street Journal, Forbes, Diversity-Inc*, NPR, the *Washington Post, Parents, Marie Claire*, and the *Los Angeles Times*. She is based in Los Angeles, California, with a global upbringing including ties to South and Southeast Asia and Canada. She is an instructor on Diversity, Equity, and Inclusion for the UCLA Post-MBA program and is coaching faculty for the Diversity, Equity, and Inclusion Coaching Center at the Forum on Workplace Inclusion and Diversity Woman conferences.

A frequently requested thought leader on DEI, race, unconscious bias, leadership, culture, and identity, Farzana is committed to helping organizations and individuals lead more effectively and is passionate about cultivating belonging in the workplace and society overall. Her book *Raising Multiracial Children: Tools for Nurturing Identity in a Racialized World* was published in 2020. For more information about Farzana's consulting services and educational resources, visit www.farzananayani.com and connect with her on social media: @farzananayani.

·ABOUT FARZANA NAYANI, CONSULTING & TRAINING ·

FARZANA NAYANI, CONSULTING & TRAINING is a certified minority- and woman-owned diversity, equity, and inclusion consulting firm headquartered in Los Angeles, California, with over 20 years of experience. The firm offers expertise from consultants from a wide array of backgrounds and expertise, from HR to organizational strategy and individualized coaching. The firm is dedicated to cultivating inclusive and equitable environments through awareness building, action, healing, and transformation, with an intersectional lens.

The vision of the company is to positively impact society for the greatest benefit to all, underscoring the uplifting of systematically excluded and historically marginalized groups. This vision is fulfilled through offering compassion, knowledge, and expertise of practices and perspectives that work to support organizations toward the greatest impact.

FARZANA NAYANI, CONSULTING & TRAINING SERVICES AND PRODUCTS INCLUDE THE FOLLOWING:

- Diversity, equity, and inclusion assessment and strategy development

- Focus groups and listening sessions

- Trainings and speaking engagements

- Executive coaching and CEO advising

- Board retreat facilitation

- Coaching programs for underrepresented groups

- Transformational healing sessions

- Intercultural Development Inventory (IDI) learning and development

- Customized solutions to address specific issues

- Digital learning products on DEI, unconscious bias, and employee resource groups

The firm's ERG Dynamics™ offerings provide educational resources and materials that help working professionals plan and lead ERG activities effectively with knowledge, sensitivity, and confidence in a constantly changing society.

For more information and resources for your employee resource group, visit http://www.ergdynamics.com.

Berrett-Koehler
Publishers

Berrett-Koehler is an independent publisher dedicated to an ambitious mission: *Connecting people and ideas to create a world that works for all.*

Our publications span many formats, including print, digital, audio, and video. We also offer online resources, training, and gatherings. And we will continue expanding our products and services to advance our mission.

We believe that the solutions to the world's problems will come from all of us, working at all levels: in our society, in our organizations, and in our own lives. Our publications and resources offer pathways to creating a more just, equitable, and sustainable society. They help people make their organizations more humane, democratic, diverse, and effective (and we don't think there's any contradiction there). And they guide people in creating positive change in their own lives and aligning their personal practices with their aspirations for a better world.

And we strive to practice what we preach through what we call "The BK Way." At the core of this approach is *stewardship,* a deep sense of responsibility to administer the company for the benefit of all of our stakeholder groups, including authors, customers, employees, investors, service providers, sales partners, and the communities and environment around us. Everything we do is built around stewardship and our other core values of *quality, partnership, inclusion,* and *sustainability.*

This is why Berrett-Koehler is the first book publishing company to be both a B Corporation (a rigorous certification) and a benefit corporation (a for-profit legal status), which together require us to adhere to the highest standards for corporate, social, and environmental performance. And it is why we have instituted many pioneering practices (which you can learn about at www.bkconnection.com), including the Berrett-Koehler Constitution, the Bill of Rights and Responsibilities for BK Authors, and our unique Author Days.

We are grateful to our readers, authors, and other friends who are supporting our mission. We ask you to share with us examples of how BK publications and resources are making a difference in your lives, organizations, and communities at www.bkconnection.com/impact.

Dear reader,

Thank you for picking up this book and welcome to the worldwide BK community! You're joining a special group of people who have come together to create positive change in their lives, organizations, and communities.

What's BK all about?

Our mission is to connect people and ideas to create a world that works for all.

Why? Our communities, organizations, and lives get bogged down by old paradigms of self-interest, exclusion, hierarchy, and privilege. But we believe that can change. That's why we seek the leading experts on these challenges—and share their actionable ideas with you.

A welcome gift

To help you get started, we'd like to offer you a **free copy** of one of our bestselling ebooks:

www.bkconnection.com/welcome

When you claim your **free ebook**, you'll also be subscribed to our blog.

Our freshest insights

Access the best new tools and ideas for leaders at all levels on our blog at ideas.bkconnection.com.

Sincerely,

Your friends at Berrett-Koehler